COMMUNIST CONTINUITY AND THE FIGHT FOR WOMEN'S LIBERATION

Part 3

Abortion Rights, the ERA, and the Rebirth of a Feminist Movement

The Party Campaigns for Women's Rights

PATHFINDER

New York   London   Montreal   Sydney

Contents

Introduction	4
by Mary-Alice Waters, July 26, 1992	
1. The abortion struggle: What have we accomplished; where should we go from here?	9
by Betsey Stone and Mary-Alice Waters	
Reprinted from SWP Discussion Bulletin, *vol. 31, no. 19, July 1973*	
2. Feminism and the Marxist movement	27
by Mary-Alice Waters	
Reprinted from Pathfinder pamphlet; originally published in *October 1972* International Socialist Review	
3. Toward a mass feminist movement	44
Resolution adopted by SWP National Convention, August 1971	
Reprinted from SWP Discussion Bulletin, *vol. 29, no. 4, April 1971*	
4. Emergence of a new feminist movement	62
Excerpt from 'Perspectives and Lessons of the New Radicalization,' political resolution adopted by the SWP National Convention, August 1971	
Reprinted from A Revolutionary Strategy for the 70s: Documents of the Socialist Workers Party	
5. Struggles by women reflect the depth of the social crisis and radicalization	64
Excerpts from 'Prospects for Socialism in America,' political resolution adopted by SWP National Convention, August 1975	
Reprinted from The Changing Face of U.S. Politics: The Proletarian Party and the Trade Unions	
From Part IV: 'Changing Character and Composition of the Working Class'	64
From Part V: 'Radicalization and Mobilization of the Allies of the Proletariat'	64
6. The fight for an independent women's movement	67
Report adopted by SWP National Committee, February 25, 1978, by Willie Mae Reid	
Reprinted from Party Organizer, *vol. 2, no. 3, May 1978*	
Appendix: April 1977 National NOW Conference	
2,000 feminists debate strategy for movement, by Nancy Cole	82
Reprinted from the Militant, *May 6, 1977*	
SWP answers red-baiting, by Mary-Alice Waters	87
Reprinted from the Militant, *May 6, 1977*	

7. Campaigning for the ERA

(a) Impact of July 9, 1978, 100,000-strong march on Washington
for the ERA and the perspectives for NOW   91
Report adopted by SWP Political Bureau, November 3, 1978, by Wendy Lyons
Reprinted from Party Organizer, *vol. 2, no. 8, November 1978*

(b) Labor for Equal Rights Now (LERN) and
the Illinois ERA campaign   99
Report adopted by SWP national steelworkers fraction, February 24, 1980, by Pat Grogan
Reprinted from Party Organizer, *vol. 4, no. 1, April 1980*

(c) Mortal blow to the ERA: NOW leadership capitulates
to Washington's third militarization drive   105
***Excerpt from report on 'Imperialist Militarization and the Draft,' adopted by
SWP National Committee, May 25, 1980, by Andrea Morell***
Reprinted from Party Organizer, *vol. 5, no. 2 April 1981*

Introduction

by Mary-Alice Waters

From Wichita to Buffalo, from Boston to Milwaukee, from New Orleans to New York, a new generation of women is taking to the streets to defend women's rights. A new fighting layer of the working class is learning to see the defense of these rights as inseparable from defending the democratic rights of all and the class interests of workers.

As thousands of women come to recognize the need to *act* to prevent hard-fought gains from being lost, they are rejecting the myth that the oppression of women as a sex was vanquished by the "second wave" of the feminist movement in the early 1970s. They are confronting all the fundamental questions that previous generations of women fighting for their liberation have addressed, and that the working-class vanguard must answer if it is to advance toward socialism.

Why are women oppressed? How did that oppression begin? Why are opponents of a woman's right to choose and of the Equal Rights Amendment so determined to perpetuate laws and customs that deny women an equal role in society? Who benefits? What social forces have the power to end the second-class status of women, and have common interests in the fight for women's liberation?

These three Education for Socialists bulletins—which bear the common title *Communist Continuity and the Fight for Women's Liberation: Documents of the Socialist Workers Party, 1971–86* aim to make available raw materials that will help the generation of women and men now joining battle in defense of women's rights find the answers to these and similar questions and win them to the communist movement.

The bulletins should be read as a "work in progress." They draw together in one place some of the most important resolutions, reports, and articles that come out of the active involvement of the Socialist Workers Party and Young Socialist Alliance in the fight for women's rights since a new feminist movement arose at the end of the 1960s. A product of the deep-going economic and social changes that began with Washington's preparations for entry into World War II, the "second wave" of feminism was one of the powerful components of the radicalization of the 1960s and 1970s that profoundly affected the working class and changed political consciousness on an even broader scale.

Part I of the series, *Women's Liberation and the Line of March of the Working Class,* contains the main programmatic documents, or articles and reports based on them, that have been adopted by the Socialist Workers Party since 1979. Central to this bulletin is the resolution "Socialist Revolution and the Struggle for Women's Liberation," adopted by the SWP convention in August 1979. The resolution in its final form was the product of collective discussion and debate in the international movement the SWP was part of at that time, the Fourth International, and is enriched by the varied experiences in many countries it incorporates. The initial drafting of the resolution, however, as well as the final editing, was done by the leadership of the SWP. While one or two points would be developed differently if written today, and others added, the resolution remains the best guide we have on the central place and weight of the fight for women's liberation in the strategic line of march of the working class toward socialism.

Other materials in Part I develop specific points that are incorporated in the international resolution. The excerpts from other reports often explain at greater length or more clearly how we arrived at some of the conclusions that are codified in the resolution.

"The Capitalist Ideological Offensive against Women Today" builds on the international resolution to take up a number of important questions that came to the fore in the early 1980s. It is excerpted from the introduction to the book *Cosmetics, Fashions, and the Exploitation of Women;* that introduction was based on a report adopted by the SWP National Committee entitled "Confronting the Leadership Pressures on Women during a Retreat of the Labor Movement," which is contained in Part II of this series.

All of the material in Part I registers the political conquests of the SWP since the late 1970s, as the party cadres deepened their orientation toward the industrial working class and unions, building a party that is proletarian not only in its program and perspectives but overwhelmingly in its composition, political milieu, and rhythms of activity as well. As part of that process, deepening our understanding of the character and central importance of the fight to end women's oppression as a sex was indispensable.

Reading this material together with the SWP resolutions and reports contained in *The Changing Face of U.S. Politics: The Proletarian Party and the Trade Unions,* published by Pathfinder Press, will place it in an even broader national and international class framework. The women involved in the work documented in these bulletins were the same women who were advancing the fights in their plants and unions and in the broader working-class movement. And they were changing themselves and their party in the process.

The documents in Part II, *Women, Leadership, and Proletarian Norms of the Communist Movement,* register the party's political progress as we conquered the kinds of working-class attitudes and norms of functioning that make it possible for workers, members of oppressed nationalities, and women to develop as party leaders. The ability of the Socialist Workers Party cadres to discuss objectively and lead politically on the range of questions documented here has been unique in the communist movement. These questions include:
• the need for affirmative action within the party;
• why quotas, exclusive caucuses, and exclusionary social activities are destructive to comradely relations and leadership development in a revolutionary centralist working-class organization;
• eradicating the cancer of race-baiting;
• establishing that violence of any kind against women destroys party democracy and political equality and is incompatible with membership;
• helping members with children maximize their political activity, without pretending the party can or should take responsibility for child care.

The SWP has conquered these proletarian norms and rejected the petty-bourgeois attitudes and functioning prevalent in other organizations that pretend to speak in the interests of the working class. Had we not been able to do so, the SWP too would have been torn apart in petty factional battles and clique fights similar to those that have decimated the Communist Party, among others, in recent years.

Part III of the series is entitled *Abortion Rights, the ERA, and the Rebirth of a Feminist Movement: The Party Campaigns for Women's Rights.* It contains the resolution adopted by the SWP in 1971, the first party convention after the mass movement for women's liberation burst on the political scene; it registers the party's enthusiastic support for, and involvement in, that revolutionary development. While this might seem unremarkable today, at the time it set the SWP apart from virtually all other working-class organizations.

Part III also contains "Feminism and the Marxist Movement," which took up and answered the challenge of the "socialist-feminist" currents that emerged as part of the new radicalization. These currents decried the supposed theoretical inadequacies of Marxism and argued the need for a new theoretical framework to chart a course toward women's liberation.

The core of Part III, however, documents the work of the Socialist Workers Party and Young Socialist Alliance to build the abortion rights movement in the early 1970s and, a few years later, to mobilize the kind of movement that would have been necessary to win the Equal Rights Amendment to the U.S. Constitution. These reports and articles draw together the work we were part of and capture the campaigning, interventionist spirit of the party and youth; they provide the best guide for today, as we respond to the new struggles that are unfolding.

As we collectively read, study, discuss, and use this material, we will gain a better appreciation of what is most valuable in preparing us to participate in today's struggles. We will also better understand the accomplishments and conquests of the battles that have brought us this far.

In bringing these documents together, no attempt has been made to edit them in light of later experience or to change formulations or points in early documents that are clarified and explained more accurately in later materials. Readers will be able to see for themselves the evolution of the party's collective thinking and growing political comprehension of a range of questions.

JULY 26, 1992

Contents of Part I

Part I—women's liberation and the line of march of the working class

Introduction
by Mary-Alice Waters, July 26, 1992

1. The capitalist ideological offensive against women today
***Excerpt from introduction to* Cosmetics, Fashions, and the Exploitation of Women**
by Mary-Alice Waters, November 1985

2. The struggle by women against their oppression as a sex is a form of the class struggle
Report adopted by the National Convention of the Socialist Workers Party, August 7, 1979
by Mary-Alice Waters

Reprinted from International Internal Discussion Bulletin, *vol. XVI, no. 6, October 1979*

3. Socialist revolution and the struggle for women's liberation
Resolution adopted by the National Convention of the Socialist Workers Party, August 7, 1979

Reprinted from 1979 World Congress of the Fourth International: Major resolutions and reports, *special supplement to* Intercontinental Press

4. Social weight and revolutionary strategy for the transformation of the labor movement
Excerpt from report adopted by SWP National Committee, April 29, 1979
by Jack Barnes

From 'A new stage of revolutionary working-class politics,' from Part II: 'The roots of revolutionary strategy.' Reprinted from The Changing Face of U.S. Politics: The Proletarian Party and the Trade Unions

5. Affirmative action gains for women in industry and the way forward for the women's movement
Excerpt from report adopted by SWP National Committee, April 29, 1979
by Jack Barnes

From 'A new stage of revolutionary working-class politics,' from Part III: 'Resolving the crisis of proletarian leadership.' Reprinted from The Changing Face of U.S. Politics: The Proletarian Party and the Trade Unions

Contents of Part II

Part II—Women, leadership, and proletarian norms of the communist movement

1. **Confronting the leadership pressures on women during a retreat of the labor movement**
   Report on 'Preparing the election of the National Committee,' adopted by SWP National Committee, May 1985
   by Mary-Alice Waters
   Reprinted from Information Bulletin *no. 2 in 1985, June 1985*

2. **Forging the leadership of a proletarian party**
   Excerpt from report adopted by SWP National Committee, May 1979
   by Mary-Alice Waters
   Reprinted from SWP Discussion Bulletin, *vol. 36, no. 13, July 1979*

3. **Leading the party into industry**
   Excerpt from report adopted by SWP National Committee, February 1978
   by Jack Barnes
   Reprinted from Party Organizer, *vol. 2, no. 2, April 1978*

4. **Violence against women is incompatible with party membership**
   Excerpt from 'Political Committee report on Control Commission recommendations,' report adopted by SWP National Convention, August 13, 1977
   by Linda Jenness
   Reprinted from Internal Information Bulletin *no. 7 in 1977, September 1977*

5. **Communist norms and nonexclusive social affairs**
   Report adopted by SWP National Convention, August 13, 1977
   by Catarino Garza
   Reprinted from Internal Information Bulletin *no. 7 in 1977, September 1977*

6. **Race-baiting and communist leadership**
   Report adopted by SWP National Committee, February 1986
   by Mac Warren
   Reprinted from Information Bulletin *no. 1 in 1986, April 1986*

7. **Children, child care, and membership norms of a proletarian party**
   Report adopted by SWP Political Committee, June 18, 1986
   by Jack Barnes
   Reprinted from Information Bulletin *no. 2 in 1986, August 1986*

   Appendix 1:
   Letter to Political Committee from James, June 12, 1986
   Letter to Political Committee from Vivian, June 6, 1986
   Reprinted from Information Bulletin *no. 2 in 1986, August 1986*

   Appendix 2:
   Excerpt from report on women's liberation movement
   From report adopted by SWP National Committee, March 14, 1971
   by Betsey Stone
   Reprinted from Internal Information Bulletin *no. 2 in 1971, April 1971*

THE ABORTION STRUGGLE: WHAT HAVE WE ACCOMPLISHED; WHERE SHOULD WE GO FROM HERE?
Reprinted from 'SWP Discussion Bulletin,' Vol. 31, No. 19, July 1973

by Betsey Stone and Mary-Alice Waters

The January 1973 Supreme Court decision legalizing abortion was a landmark victory in the struggle for women's liberation.

It was the first major advance recorded by the new wave of struggles by women in the fight against the institutionalized domestic slavery to which women have been relegated by class society.

The abortion rights victory opened the door for millions of women—especially working women, Blacks, Chicanas, Puerto Ricans—to begin to control their own reproductive functions, their own bodies. It went a significant way towards establishing a fundamental human right for all women—the right to choose whether or not to bear a child.

Freedom from enforced motherhood is a precondition to women's liberation. Only with the right to control their own bodies can women begin to reassert their full human identity as productive, not only reproductive, beings.

The 1973 abortion rights decision sets the stage for a new level of women's liberation struggles. Such struggles will be inspired by the victory won and enhanced by the heightened social expectations and confidence of women developed because of the decision and the changes it will bring.

The victory can only serve to hasten the development of a proletarian vanguard of fighting women and men capable of achieving women's liberation and leading the American socialist revolution to victory.

The Socialist Workers Party made a contribution in helping to win the abortion rights victory. The purpose of this article is to draw a balance sheet of the party's women's liberation activity since the last convention, most importantly our participation in this fight to repeal capitalism's reactionary abortion laws. The article will also assess the development of the feminist movement over the past four years, the present state of the struggle, and our tasks in the period ahead.

The Political Committee does not plan to present a draft resolution to the convention, or to propose a separate agenda point on women's liberation work. We hope this contribution will facilitate the discussion which will take place under the political report and at the panel on women's liberation work.

Behind the Supreme Court victory

The Supreme Court decision was brought about by a combination of factors. Some of them are cited in the 1971 SWP resolution, "Towards a Mass Feminist Movement," as factors responsible for the emergence of the women's liberation struggle as a whole.

First, the decision was a product of the increasing disparity between the actual position of women and the possibilities provided by today's technology and wealth for freeing women from a narrow existence of domestic drudgery. As a result of psychological conditioning and economic coercion women continue to be channeled into the role of wife-mother-housekeeper. They are systematically molded for this socially prescribed role by law, by custom, by religion, by the dominant ideology of the ruling class. They are taught it is their "natural" place. While women today have more options than ever before in terms of jobs, education, and participation in productive activity, they are still restricted at every turn by the institutionalized forms of sexual discrimination and oppression which are the basic underpinnings of class society.

This disparity between what is and what could be became abundantly clear in the debate around the issue of abortion. The use of birth control devices and the pill are now widespread in the U.S., and are recognized as a legal right in most states. Under modern medical practice abortions are safer by far than childbirth. But for simply exercising the right to control their own bodies, women have been branded as criminals and condemned to risk their lives at the hands of backstreet abortionists.

This and similar contradictions gave rise to the women's liberation movement in general and the struggle against the reactionary abortion laws in particular.

The impact of women's liberation ideas and the fight carried out by large numbers of women was another major factor behind the Supreme Court decision. This was manifested in the fact that the concept put forward by large numbers of women's liberation forces—that abortion should be a woman's right to choose—was incorporated in the Supreme Court decision.

The ruling was also influenced by the general radicalization with its challenges to traditional attitudes and values. The rise of the Black movement, the antiwar movement and other struggles for social change helped create an atmosphere that spurred changing views on abortion.

The influence of the radicalization, and the development of the feminist movement in particular, was reflected in the polls that showed a rapid change in attitudes relating to abortion between 1968 and 1971. In 1968, the polls reported that only 15 percent of the population believed women had a right to abortion. Abortion was still largely a secret ordeal that many women went through but were afraid to talk about. By 1969, the percentage supporting abortion rose dramatically to 40 percent. By 1971, it was 50 percent.

The rise of the women's liberation movement helped bring about the first partial victory in the abortion rights struggle: the legalization of abortion in New York state in 1970. The excellent safety record in New York under the new law and the demonstrated demand for legal abortion helped legitimize the procedure and also made it more difficult for the ruling class to take back this limited gain women had won.

The liberalization of abortion in New York sparked a concerted drive by the anti-abortion forces which began to assume national scope. The polarization and ferment that began to mount over this question forced the ruling class to realize they would have to settle the matter in one way or another.

Orientation confirmed

The victory for women embodied in the Supreme Court decision confirms the orientation of the SWP of throwing its energies into the fight for the right to abortion. It showed we were correct in our insistence that the question of abortion was becoming a national political issue around which a struggle would take place which would lead to either a significant victory or a major setback for the women's liberation movement and the radicalization in general. It confirms our view that it was crucial for the feminist movement to intervene in this struggle, to fight for the interests of women and to thereby demonstrate the relevance of the women's liberation movement to the masses of women.

Although the Supreme Court decision was handed down before either the feminist movement or the abortion rights movement had reached a stage of mobilizing large numbers of women, the work we carried out as builders of the Women's National Abortion Action Coalition (WONAAC) had an important impact. Over the past several years, WONAAC has been the one women's liberation organization that has carried out consistent activity oriented toward involving women in struggle, independent of the capitalist parties and politicians, around an issue of vital concern to masses of women. It had the correct political position on abortion as a woman's right. It was the only women's liberation group to continue to fight uncompromisingly for the right to abortion throughout the 1972 election period. It was the only one to answer the so-called "right-to-life" campaign in an organized manner and on a correct political basis. And it was the group that did the most to publicize, encourage and link up with the growing international struggle for the right to abortion.

WONAAC played an important role in providing a correct perspective for the women's liberation struggle at a time when the feminist movement was facing a crisis of orientation. The full significance of this role of WONAAC and the abortion rights struggle can be best understood by looking at the origins and development of the women's liberation struggle as a whole over the past four years.

Emergence of the women's liberation movement

What has been popularly referred to as the "women's liberation movement" is not a movement in any organized sense. There has been a general radicalization of women around feminist ideas. This has reflected itself in many and varied organizational forms, from consciousness-raising groups to union caucuses, as well as in changing attitudes on a mass scale. When we talk about the women's liberation "movement," it is more accurately this general radicalization that we are referring to with its organized and unorganized reflections.

The SWP recognized the emergence of the new women's liberation movement as extremely significant in terms of its potential for affecting the course of the American socialist revolution. The explosiveness with which the movement developed around 1969, the rapidity of the spread of women's liberation ideas, and the radical nature of the movement's critique of the family and the roots of women's oppression, were seen as a reflection of the depth of the current radicalization and the deepening contradictions of American capitalism.

In its 1971 resolution "Towards a Mass Feminist Movement," the SWP noted that while struggles by women had accompanied every previous radicalization in the U.S., this new women's liberation movement was unprecedented. It states: "Never before has there been a feminist movement as irreconcilable in its opposition to oppression, as radical in its critique of the social forces that breed these inequities, and as potentially powerful a force for helping to end that oppression, as the emerging movement of today."

This new movement represented a significant expansion of the general radicalization process affecting American society. It meant people were beginning to challenge some of the most ingrained prejudices and basic institutions upholding capitalist society.

While the emergence of the women's liberation movement was fundamentally conditioned by the growth of objective contradictions in the situation of women, it was also an outgrowth of the general radicalization developing in American society. The particular forms the movement took and the way it developed were influenced by the specific nature and stage of the general radicalization.

The feminist movement was born at the height of the ferment of the rising antiwar struggle in 1968–70. The movement was also deeply inspired by the Black liberation struggle and the fury expressed in the ghetto rebellions that swept the country in the mid-1960s.

In this context of general questioning of authority and challenges to the status quo, hundreds of women's liberation groups sprang up throughout the country in 1969, most of them beginning as consciousness-raising groups. Numerous conferences were organized to discuss and formulate demands relating to women's oppression. There was an outpouring of literature by women examining the nature of sexist oppression and how to end it.

This initial flowering of the movement culminated in the giant outpouring on August 26, 1970, the 50th anniversary of the winning of women's suffrage. In New York, where the largest demonstration took place, 30,000 were in the streets. The unexpected size of these demonstrations is partly explained by the fact that they followed on the heels of the largest student upsurge in American history—the May 1970 explosion after the invasion of Cambodia and the murder of the Kent State and Jackson State students.

As an outgrowth of the general youth radicalization of the 1960s, the women's liberation movement reflected the weaknesses and limitations of that radicalization as well as the strengths. As happened with the antiwar and Black movements, the feminist movement very quickly faced a crisis of orientation. Given the relative political quiescence of the labor movement and the absence of a mass revolutionary socialist party, there were strong tendencies toward ultraleftism, sectarianism, workerism, reformism, and other attempts to find shortcuts to move the struggle forward.

Many of the women who were initiators of the women's liberation groups came out of Students for a Democratic Society (SDS) or the antiwar movement as conscious opponents of any attempt to build a mass action movement. Many in this layer looked to the women's movement as a way out of political activity and as an escape from the kind of political struggle that characterized the antiwar movement and the student movement.

From the very beginning these ex-New-Left currents attempted to steer the women's movement in the direction of ultraleftism, elitism, and a reliance on changing "life styles" as solutions to the oppression of women.

In addition, the central leadership of the National Organization for Women (NOW) was a consciously reformist nucleus that worked to turn the energies of the developing women's liberation movement toward subordination to Democratic Party politics.

The August 26, 1970 demonstration provoked a deep-going debate over many of the same questions that had previously been fought out in the antiwar movement. This outpouring of protest showed the great potential before the women's liberation movement. It sharply posed the question of what strategy the movement should follow. How could this potential force of masses of women be organized and mobilized as a power to help bring about the liberation of women?

A discussion of this had already begun prior to the demonstration. In countless consciousness-raising groups, for example, women reached a point in their discussions when they realized that the consciousness-raising group was no longer adequate. They came to the conclusion that talking was not enough, that something had to be done about the oppression of women. However, most activists were not convinced of the effectiveness of any particular course of action. The questions raised—such as what is the cause of the oppression of women, who is responsible for maintaining it, and how can we end it—could only be answered by a Marxist analysis and perspective.

Our answer to the question of what direction women's liberation groups should take was that they had to turn outward, toward the masses of working women, Black, Chicana, and Puerto Rican women. We said feminists should organize around the basic issues facing the masses of women, with the aim of mobilizing women, independent of the capitalist politicians and parties, to fight for their needs. We said to free themselves women had to challenge the fundamental institutions of this society; that changing one's life style was no solution at all.

We said the women's liberation forces had to break out of any closed-circle existence and involve in struggle the many women who did not yet consider themselves feminists but were ready to fight for certain basic demands.

Debate divides the movement

The debate that broke out around the meaning of August 26 divided the movement fundamentally over the question: for or against the perspective of mass action as the indispensable form of struggle. The SWP and YSA, which had played an important role in building the August 26 demonstrations, took the lead in explaining the significance of those actions and proposing a continuation of an action perspective for the movement.

Lined up against the SWP and YSA and the independent activists who had been inspired by August 26 were three main currents:

1. One current insisted upon the overriding importance of small groups of what they considered "true feminists." Their view was that women could move toward liberation primarily by changing their own consciousness and life styles. Another aspect of this theory was a disdain for the masses of women, who were not yet "conscious feminists." One influential section of this current began to equate feminism with lesbianism and to look down upon women who were not gay as not "real" feminists.

2. The second was the liberal current. It was primarily represented by the leadership of the National Organization for Women. They tended to counterpose lobbying, "behind-the-scenes legislative action," and small "militant" acts to mass action around specific issues. Immediately after sponsoring the August 26 demonstrations, the NOW leadership rejected further actions of this kind and more openly began to orient toward involvement in Democratic and Republican party politics in preparation for the 1972 elections.

3. Finally, there were the various sectarian tendencies on the left calling themselves socialist or anti-imperialist. These women tended to oppose and denigrate the August 26 actions or any other feminist action as "not radical enough." Some groupings, such as the International Socialists, enamoured of rhetoric about "orienting toward

working women," opposed any campaigns that had the potential of involving large numbers of working women.

These three currents were not totally distinct from one another. Many of the groups dominated by SDS women, for example, were characterized by both sectarianism and an orientation toward counter-life-styles.

As the debate in the movement continued through the fall and winter of 1970–71, the crisis of perspective began taking its toll. Many women's liberation groups and consciousness-raising groups which had sprung up during the earlier period became more and more introverted and apolitical. With the passage of time, most such groups completely disappeared.

To help propel the movement forward and in order to provide an orientation, the SWP proposed outward-reaching activities in the women's groups in which we were involved. However, we encountered strong resistance to this action perspective, both in NOW and in the citywide women's liberation groups, such as the New York Women's Center, Redstockings, Washington D.C. Women's Liberation, and the Chicago Women's Liberation Union, which were led, in the main, by ex-SDSers who were consciously opposed to such actions. The reformists and ultralefts more and more resorted to red-baiting as a method of combatting our political ideas.

It was at this time, when much of the organized movement was becoming introverted and clique-ridden, that struggles began to sharpen in several states around the issue of abortion. Abortion law repeal coalitions and groups sprang up in numerous states, some formed with SWP and YSA participation, others arising where we had no comrades. In the spring of 1970, the New York movement had initiated an important court suit and organized a demonstration through the coalition called People to Abolish Abortion Laws (PAAL).

Passage of the liberalized New York abortion law in March 1970 was a turning point in the struggle. At one and the same time it provided an impetus to the abortion rights fight and prompted the reactionary anti-abortion forces, spearheaded by the powerful Catholic Church hierarchy, to launch a campaign to reverse the trend toward legalization. Numerous capitalist politicians including Richard Nixon felt impelled to publicly support this reactionary offensive. Newspaper and magazine articles on the abortion question proliferated; debates raged in more and more state legislatures; meetings, rallies and demonstrations were organized by both sides in the abortion fight.

It became evident that a heated and deepening nationwide struggle was looming on this question, and that either the New York law would be reversed by the anti-abortion offensive, or legalization of abortion would be extended to other states. The fact that the reactionaries had decided to rally their forces for a showdown fight around this issue made imperative the need to organize and fight back.

Considerations behind the abortion campaign

In countering the attacks of the reactionaries, the abortion coalitions and groups around the country were handicapped by their local outlook. An effective struggle to repulse the onslaught of the reactionaries and win a decisive victory for women required a unified, nationwide effort on the part of the feminist movement.

A national action campaign centered on the abortion issue could rebuff the reactionary rightwing offensive and become the vehicle to enable the women's liberation forces to break out of a relatively closed-circle existence and begin to organize around the real social and political issues that affected the masses of women. Such a campaign could provide the opportunity to advance beyond the stage of general propagandizing about women's oppression to organizing a fight to attain a concrete goal of vital importance to masses of American women. It could begin to demonstrate, in practice, that the ideas of women's liberation are of concern to working women, Black women, Chicanas. It could be a way of involving new layers of women in the feminist movement.

The SWP considered such a campaign to be a realistic prospect because, in addition to our own movement, there were other significant forces already involved in the abortion rights struggle who would welcome the idea of a national effort on this issue. In the spring of 1971, Women vs. Connecticut, a group which sponsored a class action suit against that state's abortion law, had already called for a national march on Washington demanding repeal of the laws restricting the right of women to obtain abortions.

From the beginning, the feminist component of the abortion rights movement had been the most uncompromising in its stand for total repeal of abortion laws and the right of a woman to choose abortion. One of the dangers of the developing controversy over abortion was that the population-control advocates who were influential at this time in many pro-abortion groups would direct the debate into a losing fight over population control vs. "right-to-life." Leadership by the women's liberation movement was needed to shift the debate off this axis and squarely pose the question on the basis of a woman's right to control her own body. This was particularly important in order to involve Black, Puerto Rican, and Chicana women in the abortion struggle, since most population-control theories and proposals are marked by racist attitudes and assumptions. Clear political leadership by the feminist movement was also needed to fight liberal proposals that women should be allowed abortions only under special conditions, such as rape, incest, or threat to the life or health of the pregnant woman.

The demands embodying a clear, principled position based on a woman's right to choose were—"Repeal all anti-abortion laws" and "No forced sterilization."

A broad women's coalition, united behind these demands was needed. We supported the idea of a *women's* coalition for two reasons.

1) We agreed that women should organize themselves to fight against their oppression as women. Those who suffer directly from a particular form of exploitation, injustice or oppression will, in their overwhelming majority, be the most uncompromising in their struggle against it. Women alone cannot make a socialist revolution and establish the material prerequisites for ending their oppression. But this does not alter the fact that women must organize and lead the fight to liberate themselves. No one else can or will do it for them. Organizing women to fight on the abortion question was a way of setting an example for how women should fight, a way to provide a perspective for the entire women's liberation movement, to demonstrate in action how to struggle. A woman's coalition could help increase the confidence of women in their ability to lead, to organize, to fight and win.

2) In the absence of a mass revolutionary party, a coalition of conscious women's liberation forces, united around the demand for abortion as a woman's right, provided the strongest possible left wing of the abortion struggle. With an organized and politically clear left wing *leading* the abortion struggle, the women's liberation movement could reach out to broader forces and involve them in the abortion rights fight. This could be done with less danger of the struggle being derailed by the non-feminist and liberal forces who were not committed to fight for abortion as a woman's right.

WONAAC, the feminist coalition we helped originate, thus had a double function. First, it was a component part of the women's liberation movement, an expression of the rising militancy and determination of significant numbers of women to fight for their liberation. It provided a focus, a perspective and an example of how to wage that struggle.

Secondly, WONAAC was a bridge to, and provided leadership for, other non-feminist forces, both women and men, who were willing to join in the fight on a specific issue of women's oppression. WONAAC reached out to unions, women's organizations, family planning centers, health organizations, church groups, the welfare rights organization, professional clubs, and many others. It was a vehicle through which feminists could provide a *class struggle* leadership to much broader social forces.

The class struggle policy that was advocated by us in the abortion fight was based on three fundamental concepts:

First is our orientation toward issues that are fundamental to the exploitation and oppression of the working class. We advance a political line and perspective that speaks to the real problems and needs of the working masses. Struggles to resolve these problems begin to challenge the interests and prerogatives of the ruling class.

Second, our class struggle policy is based on political independence from the individuals and institutions of the ruling class political apparatus—parties, politicians, legislatures, etc. We defer nothing, we subordinate nothing to the needs of any alien class interest. While capitalist politicians and others of their ilk are welcome to support our demands and our actions, they do so on our terms.

Third are the methods of struggle employed, which are proletarian methods—the use of extra-parliamentary action as opposed to reliance on the capitalist legislature. We teach the struggling masses to rely on their own strength and united power as opposed to the institutions, representatives and spokespersons of the class enemy.

What did WONAAC represent?

Together with other forces, the SWP and YSA helped initiate the Women's National Abortion Action Coalition in July of 1971.

The initial organizing efforts, including the first national WONAAC conference, were successful in involving and inspiring hundreds of women with the perspective of united action to beat back the anti-abortion forces and participation in a struggle which could register an important victory for women. At the same time, from its very inception, a debate raged within and around WONAAC between the supporters of a mass-action approach and the sectarians and liberals who saw WONAAC as a threat to their orientations.

The alternatives to mass action were posed at the various WONAAC decision-making meetings in the form of proposals to change the focus of WONAAC's activities by: (1) adding such demands as "free abortion," "free childcare centers," and "freedom of sexual expression"; (2) eliminating demonstrations; (3) concentrating on lobbying legislators or aiding Democratic or Republican party politicians who endorsed the right to abortion.

The continuing debate within WONAAC served to educate a whole layer of feminist activists about the need for an action perspective oriented toward the masses. There were several major lessons that came out of these debates and WONAAC's experience.

1) One major debate was over the importance of the abortion issue itself. Many of the women who proposed WONAAC take up other issues did so because they believed abortion was not a matter of concern to most women.

Their arguments took many forms. Just as sectarians in the antiwar movement had objected that the demand for U.S. withdrawal from Vietnam was "not radical enough," that it "wouldn't stop the seventh war from now," so too did representatives of these currents in the women's movement try to say that the demand for legal abortion was "not radical," or that the capitalist class would easily grant it and therefore it was not worth struggling for.

Some argued that the right to abortion was not of concern to working women, either because they could not afford even a legal abortion unless it was free, or because they were more interested in getting childcare centers. They argued that since the right to abortion is not a significant issue, the role of socialists or "anti-imperialists" or "real" feminists in the abortion movement should be to raise "more radical" demands, such as "free abortion on demand" and "free, 24-hour childcare centers," or "freedom of sexual expression."

The SWP rejected these arguments as did the majority of WONAAC activists. The right to abortion is a basic democratic right of women that must be wholeheartedly championed by any socialist. Under the laws in force prior to the Supreme Court decision statistics showed that one woman out of every four would have had an abortion at some time in her life. Almost every woman had been haunted by the fear of unwanted pregnancy, and the fear of having to resort to illegal, backstreet abortionists.

We pointed out that the right to legal abortion is *especially* relevant to working women, Black, Puerto Rican and Chicana women since these are the women who have the least access to birth control information and devices, and the hardest time getting safe, inexpensive abortions under illegal conditions. They account for the overwhelming majority of botched-abortion fatalities.

We saw the fight for the right to abortion as a struggle challenging one of the most important ideological props of women's oppression. Freedom to decide when or if to bear a child is necessary if women are to begin to have any control over the course of their lives. Along with "women's duties" in the home, vulnerability to unplanned pregnancy has been one of the basic "justifications" for discriminating against women in all areas, including jobs and education. It is one of the fundamental components of reactionary ideology defining women as inferior, dependent beings, whose proper place is in the home.

We believed that winning a victory on this question was possible, and that it would represent a giant step forward for the women's liberation movement. It would alleviate an important aspect of women's oppression and represent a defeat for the reactionary anti-abortion and antifeminist forces. It would lay the basis for further struggles by women.

2) The second debate was over the mass action strategy and the tactic of focusing on the single issue of legalized abortion. Opposition to the class-struggle approach was the reason why some women sought to raise other issues that would cut across concentration on legalized abortion.

Neither the socialists nor the feminists in this country "created" the abortion issue. We did not arbitrarily "decide" that repealing the abortion laws was the question on which a major fight would develop. That was dictated by social forces much stronger than us. The right to abortion had achieved prominence as a major national political issue because of the objective social factors cited above. With or without us, struggles were beginning to occur around this question.

We rejected the notion that this struggle could be made "more radical" if WONAAC raised other demands which changed the focus of the fight. The social question that had come to the fore—because of forces beyond our control—was legalized abortion, not socialized medicine as implied by those who wanted to focus on "free abortion," or gay oppression or free childcare.

The effect of adding such demands would not be "more radical" actions, but rather to let the capitalists off the hook in the real struggle developing over legalization of abortion by not bringing to bear the potential power and anger of the many women concerned about this issue.

The most radical thing WONAAC could do, we said, was to begin to affect the consciousness of the masses of working people and to mobilize significant numbers in struggle. It is only through the experience acquired through such struggle that large numbers of people will begin to understand what we already know: that much more than legalized abortion is needed to end the oppression of women. It is only when masses are in motion, engaged in struggle, that their consciousness begins to undergo a qualitative change. Until such motion develops and unfolds according to the dynamics of mass struggles, it is nothing but ultraleftism and sectarianism to proclaim the need for struggle around "more radical" demands.

Actually the proposals to add other demands to WONAAC's program were presented not out of concern for winning those demands, but rather as a ploy to mask opposition to an effective mass-oriented campaign to win the right to abortion. They were put forward by sectarians and counterculture-oriented forces who were either opposed to building mass actions or lacked any conception of how to do so. None of these forces tried to build fights around the demands they raised.

Those who fought hardest for the demand "freedom of sexual expression," for example, were women who viewed changing their own consciousness and lifestyle as the way to win liberation. Their insistence that the abortion campaign also deal with gay oppression reflected their desire to keep the movement small and "pure" and demonstrated their lack of interest in reaching out to nonfeminist women and involve them in struggle.

The bankruptcy of the sectarians and "living room feminists" was clearly manifested during the 1972 election period. Immediately after WONAAC was formed, most of the women in the feminist movement began to look toward the 1972 elections with illusions that "lesser-evil" politics was the way to win gains.

When McGovern repudiated the abortion rights demand and the reformists were telling women to "put the abortion issue on the back burner," and to switch to "quiet, behind-the-scenes lobbying action," the sectarians and "living room feminists" offered no struggle alternative, and generally ended up supporting "lesser evil" capitalist politicians.

The record of WONAAC, on the other hand, stands up well during this period. WONAAC was the only group to continue the fight independent of capitalist politicians and parties, for the right of women to abortion. WONAAC's Abortion Action Week in May 1972 and the local tribunals in the fall of 1972 were the only counter to the "right-to-life" campaign and to Nixon's and McGovern's anti-abortion statements.

'Left Critics'

Among the main proponents of the addition of "free abortion," "free childcare," "freedom of sexual expression" and other demands were the International Socialists (IS). Their conception of the role of Marxists in the abortion struggle was not to take responsibility for helping to lead and organize an effective struggle to win legalized abortion, but to act as congenital "left" oppositionists, concerned only with proving themselves "more radical" than the rest of the women involved in the struggle.

IS also advanced the most sophisticated version of the "raise other demands" position. This was their argument that WONAAC should demand free abortion because that would be the basis for continuing the struggle after abortion law repeal was won. The argument went: "Perhaps the masses of women wouldn't understand or agree, but at least a vanguard layer would have been educated about the need for free abortions and they would keep fighting." They asserted that WONAAC didn't do this out of fear of "scaring off bourgeois women" or "dividing the movement along class lines."

In reality, however, WONAAC did divide the women's liberation movement. Not according to the sociological origins of the women involved, of course, which is what the sectarians usually mean by "dividing the movement on class lines." The divisions were over the political perspective that WONAAC adopted. It was a class struggle perspective, even though that term was never used, and most women did not consciously see it that way. It was precisely because WONAAC advanced a perspective of uncompromising struggle to mobilize the masses of women to fight for social changes in their interests, and against the interests of the ruling class, that the resistance to this orientation was so bitter.

Secondly, our concern in opposing the addition of "free abortion" or some other demand was not whether it would "scare off" potential supporters. The question was what would advance the fundamental strategic goals of WONAAC. For example, we supported making the demand for "No Forced Sterilization" part of WONAAC's programmatic aims although this was unacceptable to many supporters of abortion law repeal.

In determining what demands to raise, the question that must always be answered is: at this time, and in this political situation, what are the demands which meet the objective needs of the masses and advance the struggle, even if they are not yet fully understood. Answering that question correctly is the art of politics.

The correct answer to that question in 1971, in the women's liberation movement, was the demand to legalize abortion, and that correctly became the axis of the struggle.

Thirdly, it is sheer idealism to believe that all that is necessary to keep a campaign or mobilization going after the issue that brought it into being has been settled is to raise a "more advanced" demand. We don't arbitrarily pick the issues around which people will mobilize. In 1971 there was no reason to single out free abortion or free medical care, as opposed to childcare or some other demand, as the issue around which women would be mobilized in struggle following a victory for legalized abortion. Such questions are not predictable.

As for the question of how best to relate to the women who were the most open to radical ideas, we thought it was necessary to educate them on much more than just free abortion. We put forward our entire program of revolutionary Marxism, and our strategy for mobilizing and leading the masses of working people in struggle. We did that partially in action through WONAAC, and we did it in propaganda through the *Militant*, *ISR*, the *Young Socialist*, our forums, classes, election campaigns, etc. The result was that we won to the YSA and SWP hundreds of women—a much more important factor in continuing the struggle for women's liberation than if we had simply educated them about free abortion on demand.

3) A third dispute in WONAAC was over the policy of non-exclusion. From its very inception, all opponents of WONAAC's action program joined in a vicious red-baiting campaign reminiscent of those we experienced in the Black movement and the early period of the antiwar movement. The red-baiting was directed against WONAAC, the SWP and the YSA. Its aim was to camouflage differences with WONAAC's mass action perspective, and with the policies of the SWP and YSA in the

women's liberation movement, by scare tactics designed to frighten women away from even considering these views. The smears against WONAAC and the SWP ranged from a public red-baiting press conference held by opponents of WONAAC immediately following the founding conference of the coalition, to unrestrained red-baiting at the WONAAC conferences themselves, to attacks on WONAAC and the SWP on the floor of the 1971 NOW convention. Numerous slanderous articles and dossiers against the SWP were circulated throughout the movement. Some of the red-baiting was obviously the work of ultra-right, antifeminist forces seeking to divide and discredit the entire movement. These included an attack on WONAAC in Phillip Abbott Luce's "Pink Sheet on the New Left," and the anonymous red-baiting letter sent to reporters and speakers who had agreed to address the November 20 WONAAC demonstration in Washington, D.C.

WONAAC set an example for the movement by rebutting the attempts to weaken and divide the movement in this manner. The majority of independent activists at WONAAC's decision-making meetings reacted by insisting instead on free and fair debate of the political questions involved, and complete democracy in the movement. WONAAC refused to buckle under the red-baiting pressure, and refused to take any measures to exclude socialists or to make socialists second-class members of the coalition. If WONAAC had succumbed to these red-scare tactics, it would have provided the opponents of abortion law repeal with a weapon to destroy the left wing of the movement.

Balance sheet of the abortion campaign

In supporting the idea of building a national abortion law repeal campaign, the SWP envisioned the potential for a movement of significant proportions around this question. In drawing the balance sheet of this campaign, we must examine WONAAC's accomplishments, as well as discuss why no massive mobilizations on the abortion question developed.

The most dramatic proof of WONAAC's correctness was the Supreme Court decision itself. The ruling reflected the social impact of the burgeoning women's liberation movement as a whole. It was also affected by WONAAC's arguments and activities. The political concept that WONAAC fought for as the axis of the abortion struggle was incorporated into the decision itself with the recognition of abortion as a woman's right.

WONAAC's direct achievements are impressive. It carried out the November 20, 1971 Washington demonstration, the first national action for the right to abortion. It carried out manifold activities in local areas in May 1972. The New York WONAAC demonstration held during that Abortion Action Week was the only visible protest action by the abortion rights movement to offset the nearly successful attempts by the anti-abortion forces to have the New York abortion law repealed.

WONAAC's three national conferences served to unite large sections of the movement for valuable discussions of political questions, priorities, and exchanges of experiences in the abortion rights struggle. The largest conference in Boston attracted 1300 women. The WONAAC newsletter played an important role in giving national direction and inspiration to the abortion fight as well as providing a forum for discussion.

The coalition organized the successful defense of Shirley Wheeler, the first woman tried and convicted in the U.S. for having an abortion. It spurred the rest of the movement to join in this defense effort.

WONAAC encouraged and helped to draft the Abortion Rights Act introduced into Congress by Bella Abzug. It helped initiate class action suits in several states, including California, Massachusetts, and Michigan. It educated around the questions of availability of birth control, and of the practice of forced sterilization and polemicized against those who viewed abortion as a "population control" issue. WONAAC supporters throughout the country were the major force engaging the "right-to-life" forces in head on confrontation, rebutting their reactionary campaign in debates and literature.

Despite its limited resources, WONAAC was able to contribute to and encourage the struggle for the right to abortion in other countries. Its call for an international day of protest November 20, 1971, was answered by actions in France, England, Canada, Italy, Germany, New Zealand, and other countries. In addition, WONAAC sponsored international tours for two of its leaders, and built the International Abortion Rights Rally in March

1973 in an attempt to utilize the victory of the Supreme Court decision in this country to aid women still struggling for the right to abortion in other countries.

In addition to its contributions to the abortion rights movement, WONAAC made an important contribution in advancing the feminist struggle as a whole. It provided a medium for women's liberation activists to put their ideas into practice. It provided an example of how to struggle effectively for the needs of women and an alternative to the sterile perspectives of counterculturalism, sectarianism, reformism, and liberalism rampant in the rest of the movement.

WONAAC became a subject for discussion and debate within existing women's liberation groups including NOW, the citywide women's liberation groups and the campus groups. Although the vicious red-baiting limited WONAAC's ability to involve in action members of NOW and the citywide groups, an important layer was won over, and many campus groups wholeheartedly joined the WONAAC campaign.

WONAAC, however, was never able to involve in its activities significant numbers of women in addition to the activists of the women's liberation movement. It did not become a mass movement before the Supreme Court handed down its favorable decision. The size of WONAAC's actions were smaller than we had anticipated they would become. The reason is that we underestimated the combined impact of various obstacles to the pace of WONAAC's development. These obstacles included:

1) The intense opposition to the national abortion campaign within sections of the women's liberation movement, expressed, among other ways, in the virulent red-baiting of WONAAC. The initial strength of the ultralefts and liberals was greater than we had foreseen. We had felt that a national abortion campaign would be able to involve NOW, for example, but NOW as a national organization refused to lend its support in any effective way to the struggle for abortion. Most of the ferocity of the opposition to WONAAC came from the substantial layer of conscious opponents of a mass-action strategy both ultralefts and liberals—who had long experience in fighting against class-struggle politics in the antiwar movement and other fields.

This early period of WONAAC was similar to the early years of the antiwar movement. But unlike the antiwar movement the abortion rights victory came before WONAAC was able to harvest the fruits of the initial intense struggles over political orientation and perspective. It was only towards the end of the campaign that WONAAC began to really cut through the obstacles created by the opponents of the campaign in a significant way.

2) We underestimated the strength and effectiveness of the reactionary anti-abortion forces. The struggle for the right to abortion was a new battle, and it was up against deep-seated and widespread prejudices. The well-financed and energetic anti-abortion campaign succeeded in confusing many people over the issue, as was demonstrated in the defeat of the abortion referendums in Michigan and North Dakota.

Thus while sentiment for the right to abortion had developed rapidly, it still remained a very controversial issue. This contradictory situation was reflected in the treatment of the abortion issue by the McGovern campaign and at the Democratic Party convention. On the one hand there was for the first time a floor discussion on the abortion issue—showing the great interest that had been engendered in the issue. On the other hand, however, McGovern refused to support the right to abortion because he didn't want to antagonize the Catholic Church hierarchy, and even many pro-abortion delegates at the convention were persuaded to vote against the pro-abortion platform plank on the grounds that such a position would hurt McGovern's chances.

3) The abortion campaign was launched at the beginning of the 1972 election period, which extended over the first year and a half of WONAAC's existence. WONAAC was constantly under the pressure of the strong liberal forces who wanted to subordinate the abortion right to lesser-evil support for capitalist party candidates. The elections were an especially important factor in determining the limited amount of support WONAAC was able to gain from NOW and the Women's Political Caucus.

4) The withdrawal of U.S. troops from Vietnam and then Nixon's deal with Moscow and Peking against the Vietnamese, along with other factors enumerated in the political resolution, led to a

general downturn in the antiwar movement, and radical activities on the campuses. Just as the upsurge of the general radicalization in 1968–70 had its effect in spurring on the struggle of women, the downturn affected the movement too. In retrospect we can now see that the women's liberation movement was born at the very height of the radical upsurge of the last decade. In its struggles it was swimming upstream from the start.

During this downturn, the student movement was more susceptible to tendencies toward counterculturalism—that is, the concept that it is not necessary to change society because it is sufficient to change one's own life-style to be "liberated." These developments in the student movement reinforced similar currents in the women's movement.

All of these elements combined to slow down the pace of development of the abortion movement. There began to be a reversal of this, however, in the summer and fall of 1972 when WONAAC's campaign picked up steam. The turning point came with a number of startling successes registered by the anti-abortion forces including a "right-to-life" demonstration of 10,000 in New York, the defeat of pro-abortion referendums in Michigan and North Dakota and the near defeat of the New York law in the state legislature. These setbacks in the spring and summer of 1972, and the clear danger that the New York law would be lost during the upcoming session of the New York legislature helped convince large numbers of women of the urgent need to unite and take action to defend the gains already won and to extend them further.

As a result, WONAAC meetings and activities began to win new and broader support. The local tribunals, held in the fall of 1972, were successful in involving sectors of the women's movement and the traditional abortion rights organizations which had refused to work with WONAAC in the past.

WONAAC began to regroup broader forces that had the potential for organizing sizable actions. Three hundred people including prominent supporters of abortion in the New York Assembly and representatives from various abortion groups participated in a WONAAC-sponsored meeting in early December which mapped out plans to defend the New York law. Groups such as Planned Parenthood, the American Civil Liberties Union, the Women's Political Caucus and the National Association for the Repeal of Abortion Laws began to join with WONAAC to build specific actions. An extremely broad list of endorsements was obtained for the planned Abortion Tribunal.

WONAAC also began to work with some significant union forces, including individual union leaders of the hospital workers (Local 1199), the International Ladies Garment Workers Union, the Furrier, Leather and Machine Workers Union, the Cleaners and Dyers Joint Board, the Social Services Employees Union and others.

Although we initially misestimated the pace of WONAAC's growth and this was sometimes reflected in what we wrote in our press, WONAAC's overall impact and accomplishments confirm the general analysis and projections that led us to support and build the campaign for legalized abortion.

The dramatic upsurge of the abortion rights struggle internationally—involving demonstrations of up to 10,000 in both France and Belgium—indicates that the abortion issue does indeed have the potential, as we consistently and correctly emphasized, to provoke significant struggle for this basic need of women. It was precisely this potential that the ruling class was attempting to defuse through the concession it made with the high court ruling.

Present status of the abortion rights movement

The Supreme Court decision represented a turning point in the struggle for legalized abortion. Given the character of the decision, it will not be easy for anti-abortion forces to get it reversed. But this eventuality is by no means precluded. As we have seen in Britain, for example, reactionary forces will not and cannot give up easily on this question. In 1972, some five years after the liberalized laws went into effect there, a demonstration of 50,000 was organized by the "right-to-lifers."

The reactionary "right-to-life" forces in the U.S. have already organized considerable activity aimed at reversing the Supreme Court decision. The Catholic Church, in particular, can be counted on to continue to use its vast resources and influence in this effort. Already, eleven state legislatures have voted to support an amendment to the Constitution which would outlaw abortion. An anti-abortion conference of nearly 1,000 was held recently in Detroit. This means that supporters of the right to abortion, including WONAAC, must remain ready to respond to attempts to roll back the abortion victory.

An important element in the long-run struggle to maintain the right to abortion will be the outcome of struggles over abortion now taking place in many parts of the world. The U.S. Supreme Court decision is already having an important influence on these struggles. Similarly, we can expect that the size and outcome of the struggles abroad will have an effect on our ability to maintain legal abortion in this country.

Like other concessions won in struggle, the right to abortion will not be complete or secure until after the socialist revolution. The abortion issue rouses some of the most ingrained prejudices about women perpetrated by class society. Opposition to abortion will continue to be raised by right-wing or developing fascist movements as one of their rallying points until they are decisively defeated through a socialist revolution.

The objective situation facing the women's liberation movement

The objective contradictions to which we pointed at our last convention as underlying factors in the rise of the women's liberation movement continue to exist and in some ways have intensified. According to the 1970 census, 43.8 percent of all working-age women are now employed, and 40 percent of working women are the sole or major wage earners in their families. Working women accounted for two-thirds of the increase in total employment in the 1960s.

At the same time, the gap in pay between male and female workers has not narrowed. Women still suffer a higher unemployment rate than men, women are still kept out of the higher-paying job categories, and millions of women still receive substantially less than equal pay for equal work.

The trend toward more and more education for women continues. They received 42 percent of the bachelor degrees awarded at the end of the 1960s, and 37 percent of the masters degrees. At the same time, women face discrimination in admission standards, scholarships, and in employment and promotion in the educational system. They received only 13 percent of the doctorates, and are grossly underrepresented in all professional schools.

Moreover, while there has been a constant rise in the employment and education of women during the past decade, even these gains are not secure. As their economic situation requires, the ruling class will take whatever measures they deem necessary to try to push numbers of women out of the labor force and undermine any gains made in feminist struggles which legitimize women's participation in production on an equal basis with men.

Even in the midst of today's profits boom, the capitalists are anticipating the long run difficulties of absorbing into the workforce the large number of women who presently hold jobs. Bourgeois economists frequently point out that the present unemployment rate of five percent is not the "true" rate of unemployment since so many women are working or looking for jobs. The "real" unemployment rate they claim—for male heads of households—is much lower. There are even proposals being made to "redefine" unemployment so millions of women will not be counted.

Class society must maintain the family system as the fundamental mechanism by which class divisions are perpetuated from one generation to the next. The family system also serves as an indispensable ideological prop for an economic system based on dog-eat-dog competition and institutionalized inequality. Capitalism cannot take on the collective responsibility and social burden of childcare and integrate women into the labor force on an equal basis.

The capitalist system also gains innumerable advantages from the fact that women are an extremely flexible and malleable component of the reserve army of labor. Because of the socially accepted belief that women's "natural" place is in the home, women can be much more easily drawn into and pushed out of the labor market, according to the needs of the bosses.

The role of women as wife-mother-housekeeper —and the continued acceptance of this role by millions of men and women—is so indispensable to the capitalist rulers that they can be expected to use every possible means to try to undercut the radicalization of women. While they can be forced to give concessions like the Supreme Court ruling, they will try to chip away at whatever gains women make. This can take many forms all the way from putting economic pressure on women by limiting available childcare, to direct ideological assaults on the movement, to attacks on the legalization of abortion and the Equal Rights Amendment.

Where does the movement stand today?

In the three years since the August 26, 1970 actions, there have been no demonstrations or actions around women's liberation issues which have equaled the size or impact of August 26.

The process of disintegration of most of the women's liberation groups that began after the first spurt of the movement has also continued. Of the groups which still exist, many are concentrating on issues such as rape, prostitution and "self-help" clinics that are not central political issues to the masses of women and which do not lend themselves to effective struggle against the institutions that perpetuate women's oppression.

On the other hand, feminist sentiment and ferment continue to spread throughout the country and new layers of women have become involved in struggle. One important reflection of this is the increasingly serious coverage of women's liberation developments in the mass media and the seriousness with which Democratic and Republican party politicians are forced to treat women's issues.

Another expression of the influence of women's liberation was the number of conferences called to discuss the problems of women during the past year. Last October there was the conference of 600 predominantly Black household workers. This March the first national conference of Stewardesses for Women's Rights took place. In April some 700 Black women met in Detroit to discuss concerns of Black women. In May the California state AFL-CIO sponsored its first statewide conference of union women. This conference of about 300 adopted important resolutions, including support to low-cost childcare and support to the farmworkers organizing struggle.

Interest in women's liberation is also reflected in the success of *Ms.* magazine, which sells nearly half a million copies per month.

The campus groups, in general, do not have the dynamism or militancy which was characteristic of these groups several years ago, but campus women's liberation groups continue to exist on a relatively widespread basis and struggles around women's liberation issues keep breaking out in the high schools and colleges. There is still much potential for feminist activity on campus. Campus women's liberation groups were, in the main, responsible for organizing the impressive series of meetings and conferences in observance of this year's International Women's Day. More women's groups have been set up which are officially connected with student governments and there has been a marked growth in the numbers of women's studies departments and classes on women's history. According to an article in the March 3 *New York Times* more than 100 campuses now offer over 900 different women's studies courses.

The National Organization for Women and the Women's Political Caucus have grown. Their conferences in February were each over 2,000. NOW continues to oppose the organization of any visible mass actions but at the same time NOW's activities have not been characterized by the introverted sectarian approach of many other feminist groups and they have been able to reach out and attract new women. NOW, which claims 30,000 members, remains the largest group in the women's movement in the country.

Greater participation of Black and working women

Of special importance has been the greater involvement over the past year of Black women and working women in struggle around feminist issues. Significant protests by Black, Puerto Rican and other working women have taken place in New York, Michigan, Oregon, Pennsylvania, California and Illinois over Nixon's cutbacks in childcare services. Another important area of women's struggle has been the involvement of women in strikes or as supporters of strikes. The majority of strikers at Farah pants company are Chicanas, and women in Houston played an important role in building support for the Oil, Chemical and Atomic Workers strike.

Another indication of resistance to job discrimination has been the thousands of individual working women who have taken advantage of legal openings to fight for their rights. There has continued to be a sharp rise in complaints of sex discrimination on the job, for example. Charges brought before the Equal Employment Opportunity Commission increased from 33,000 in the year ending June 30, 1972, to some 52,000 in the current fiscal year. In addition, since 1970, class action suits on sex discrimination in education have been filed against some 10 percent of the 2,556 colleges and universities in the country.

The most dramatic result in antidiscrimination suits was the settlement made in January, 1973 with Bell Telephone in which the company was forced to pay $38 million in back pay and raises to women employees as well as Black and Spanish-speaking employees.

In the electrical industry and the communications industry the issue of maternity rights has been raised. It is also significant that the Equal Rights Amendment has begun to gain more support in the unions. In Ohio, a group of women unionists organized into the Cleveland Council of Union Women have been very aggressive in publicizing the fact that there is significant union support for the ERA and in fighting to increase that support.

A contradiction facing the feminist movement

While the questions and demands raised by the feminist movement pose fundamental challenges to the basic institutions of class society and cannot be resolved without a revolutionary struggle of the working class to destroy capitalism, the labor movement itself is not yet taking the road of independent political struggle.

This contradiction has marked the rise and evolution of the women's liberation movement, just as it has affected the radicalization as a whole. It is reflected in the fact that after the first flowering of the feminist movement in 1969–1970, the movement immediately faced a crisis of perspective. Tendencies toward counterculturalism, workerism, ultraleftism, sectarianism and reformism which developed as women tried to find some short-term solution to this contradiction were exacerbated.

This fact in no way implies that women should wait until the labor movement goes into action, or postpone struggles for demands which concern them. On the contrary, by taking the lead in fighting for their needs the women's liberation movement can help accelerate the radicalization and politicization of the labor movement. But the seemingly overwhelming task of winning liberation and the fact that there is no manifestation at present of the type of social power it will take to challenge the institutions responsible for women's oppression, encourages ultraleftism and sectarianism and the tendency of women to seek personal solutions which, they hope, will at least make life in a sexist society a little more bearable.

The fact that there is no labor party, Black party or mass revolutionary socialist party means that the capitalists have a virtual political monopoly in this country. This, of course, also strengthens reformist tendencies who want to orient the movement toward lobbying and toward support for the capitalist party politicians. It means that during election periods, feminist sentiment is expressed in the political arena mainly through attempts to fight for reforms in the Democratic and Republican parties.

A significant number of women in the feminist movement correctly see the need for action by the labor movement in support of women's needs. But they often do not understand that the objective situation places limits on the pace at which working-class struggles will develop. They look for shortcuts around this obstacle and try to "spark" working women into action. Under these conditions a certain number of radicals are inevitably drawn toward our various opponents because of the "workerist" positions they all hold to one degree or another.

The most extreme workerist tendencies such as the Workers League or Progressive Labor deny the validity of any struggles by women against their oppression as women. The only activities by women that are worthy of support, in their opinion, are struggles of women as workers, on the job. They reject the possibility that struggles by women might play an important role in the radicalization and politicization of the working class.

Others, uncomfortable about the fact that large numbers of working-class women are not marching in the streets, immediately jump to the conclusion that the problem is a subjective one—that the correct demands are not being raised. All that is necessary is a new gimmick. If we would just stop fighting around a single demand and add free abortion, free 24-hour childcare, and equal pay, working women will flock to our banner. The *Guardian* tends to advocate this approach.

Such gimmicks were similar to some of the schemes suggested by the *Guardian* to overcome problems faced by the antiwar movement. Many radicals were concerned, for example, that large numbers of Blacks did not participate in the antiwar actions. The *Guardian* said the problem was that the antiwar movement wasn't making racism one of its central issues. But as the massive Chicano antiwar actions subsequently proved, the problem did not lie in the character of the antiwar movement, but in the crisis of leadership in the Black community. The *Guardian*'s error was in underestimating the national question and thinking that the Black masses would begin to move without their own leadership.

Simply throwing out more and more demands won't move a struggle forward or bring the working class or the labor movement into motion. If that were the case, the Trotskyist movement has a better list of demands than anyone else. Our opponents could simply throw in the towel now.

The Communist Party is another group that hides behind workerist formulations. They do so to cover their reformist abstention from the women's liberation movement.

All these groups and currents end up by actually opposing those struggles taking place which can begin to have a real effect on the working masses.

The interrelationship between feminist and class struggles

The significance of the feminist struggles taking place today, and the role of socialists in building these struggles, can be best understood by looking at both the potential impact and logic of the feminist movement as well as its present contradictions. Although it is impossible to jump over the objective situation and artificially spark masses of working people into motion, the spread of feminist ideas and struggles is today having an impact on the consciousness of the working masses and will have an important effect on working-class struggles as they develop.

One current example of this is the fight by Cleveland Typographical Union local 53 to organize the unorganized workers, many of them women, in the printing and publishing industry in Northwest Ohio. The militancy of the women workers involved, who are helping set an example of how to strengthen the union by organizing along industrial lines, is a reflection of the new confidence many women workers have gained as a result of the rise of feminism.

Another indication of how the feminist movement will affect the struggles of working people was the participation of women, many of them housewives who had never been involved in a struggle of this type before, in the meat boycott. The more prominent role of Chicanas and Black women in the fight for Black and Chicano liberation is another indication of how feminism will be reflected in the class and national struggles which arise. Feminism will help to deepen the militancy of these struggles, to sharpen their political thrust, and to strengthen the side of the working class.

The struggles waged by working women and women of the oppressed nationalities over such feminist issues as childcare, abortion, equal rights on the job, equal education and paid maternity leave will be a powerful impetus to the involvement of working women—and men—in revolutionary struggle to bring down the capitalist system.

Women's liberation issues will be important in the development of a class struggle left wing in the unions and will play a role in the fight to transform the unions into revolutionary instruments of class struggle.

We cannot predict the forms or pace of development of future struggles by masses of women. But we can say that such struggles will be related to and interconnected with general upsurges of the working class, the Black movement, the Chicano movement, and youth radicalization. At the same time they will have their own unique dynamic, their own demands, their own organizational forms. They will often leap ahead of other struggles, showing the way, and drawing other forces behind them.

Our tasks in the period ahead

At the present time there is no single women's liberation issue which is a national focus for united activity of women's liberation forces. Instead, there are a number of issues around which struggles have taken place, with the issues often varying from city to city. While the nature of our participation in women's liberation struggles will be determined by political developments on a national and local scale, political decisions about how to intervene, and around what issues, will take a greater degree of branch leadership then when we had a central national campaign.

There are several issues that will continue to be of particular importance in the coming period. These are abortion, childcare, and the Equal Rights Amendment.

Abortion

As shown by the anti-abortion counteroffensive since the Supreme Court decision, the battle for the right to abortion is not over in this country. The women's liberation movement has to remain ready to take action in response to those who are fighting to chip away at, and ultimately reverse, the Supreme Court ruling. WONAAC will have a key role to play in this regard. We will want to continue supporting the actions organized by WONAAC against efforts to overturn and undermine the court decisions or to limit the right to abortion in various ways—such as stipulations that hospitals are not required to perform abortions, or various restrictive regulations like requirements for parental or husband's consent.

Childcare

A significant number of militant struggles have already taken place across the country protesting the government cutbacks of funds for childcare. Some of them succeeded in preventing childcare centers from being closed down for a while. They involved many new women in struggle, especially young working mothers. We must participate in these fights wherever they arise, attempting to extend and broaden them to whatever extent possible. The San Francisco childcare referendum is an example of one way this can be done.

Along with developing debates and struggles over childcare, we can expect a campaign of opposition by rightwing forces—just as in the struggles for the right to abortion and for the ERA. An important task will be to help educate—through our press, our election campaigns, and our participation in childcare struggles—about the importance of quality childcare to both women and children.

Equal Rights Amendment

The Equal Rights Amendment has become a national issue. It will become a test of strength between the women's liberation forces and our most reactionary opponents. Because of the broad implications of the ERA as a statement of the principle of women's equality, the outcome of this battle will have an impact on all struggles by women—for childcare, equal pay, and equal opportunities in all areas.

One of the main obstacles to building support for the ERA has been the opposition of the AFL-CIO bureaucracy to the amendment. We must continue to explain our view of the necessity to fight *both* for the extension to men of those protective labor laws that are beneficial *and* for passage of the ERA. In unions where we have members or supporters, we should attempt to initiate discussion around motions to endorse the ERA and to pass resolutions of support like those already adopted by the UAW, the Teamsters and AFSCME. The endorsement of the amendment by the May conference of the Coalition of Black Trade Unionists is a sign of the possibilities for support in the union movement for the ERA. The fight to defeat the union bureaucracies on this question will help set the stage for further struggles for equal pay and other demands of women workers.

In addition to these three questions, others have arisen in local areas. The issues around which women are challenging their oppression have proliferated. Antidiscrimination fights, struggles by working women for maternity leaves, conferences of women, support for strikes by women workers—these and others are the kinds of struggles we should become involved in. We have to keep our eyes open for possibilities to participate in struggles that have the potential to involve new layers of women in action.

Campus women's groups and NOW
The campus continues to be a place where it is possible to carry out consistent women's liberation activity and where there is the greatest interest in feminist and socialist ideas. We will want to continue to support the YSA's efforts to build general women's liberation groups on the campuses where possible. One important aspect of the activities of campus women's groups should be to build support for off-campus struggles, such as for childcare, defending the right to abortion, and the ERA. In addition, we want to participate in education and action campaigns for the needs of campus women, such as demands for health care, women's studies programs, or fights against discrimination on the campus.

We should continue our participation in NOW, as well as keeping in touch with the activities being carried on by the Women's Political Caucus. One of the important issues around which NOW has been active is the Equal Rights Amendment. In addition NOW has participated in actions around abortion, childcare, and other struggles.

In the unions
We should be alert to any opportunities to raise women's liberation issues—especially childcare, the ERA, and defense of the right to abortion—inside the trade unions and involve union women and men in supporting these struggles. In addition, we want to show our support for—and participate in, wherever possible—struggles around women's issues that arise within the unions. Examples are struggles for maternity leave rights, for preservation of beneficial protective laws and their extension to male workers, equal pay fights, and strikes and organizing campaigns by women workers.

Black, Chicana and Puerto Rican women
All of the basic demands of the women's movement have particular relevance to women of the oppressed nationalities and special efforts should be made to involve Black, Chicana and Puerto Rican women in struggles which arise around these demands. We want to pay particular attention to the issues that have involved large numbers of Black, Puerto Rican and Chicana women in struggle. These include the fight for childcare, welfare rights issues, and the right for decent pay and working conditions for household workers.

We should attempt to involve Black organizations in supporting women's liberation issues. Also, we want to be champions of the rights of Black women, Chicanas, and Puerto Rican women to full and equal participation inside the various Black, Raza and Puerto Rican organizations. The demands of women for full rights within the organizations of the oppressed nationalities has come up within La Raza Unida Party and also more recently in regard to African Liberation Day activities.

Socialist propaganda and education
One of the characteristics of the women's liberation movement has always been the widespread desire for knowledge about the basic causes of the oppression of women and how to end it. Marxists are the only ones who have answers to the very fundamental questions posed by the feminist movement concerning the basic institutions of class society and there is a tremendous openness within the movement to Marxist ideas. The continuing high level of interest in these questions, especially on the campuses, is demonstrated by the consistently good response to the lectures of Evelyn Reed and other party spokeswomen and the sales of our women's liberation literature.

Our socialist election campaigns will be an especially important vehicle for fighting for women's liberation and presenting our ideas concerning women's oppression. SWP candidates can set an example for women's liberation fighters by showing how to effectively answer the capitalist politicians and the reactionary opponents of abortion, childcare, and the ERA. Through our campaigns we will also be giving publicity and support to women's struggles.

Through our election campaign, selling our press and literature, through public forums and classes, we can continue to reach women activists with Marxist answers to the cause of women's oppression and how to fight it.

JULY 5, 1973

FEMINISM AND THE MARXIST MOVEMENT
Reprinted from pamphlet published by Pathfinder
Originally published in the October 1972 'International Socialist Review'
by Mary-Alice Waters

The following article is based on a speech given at the Socialist Activists and Educational Conference held in Oberlin, Ohio, August 13–20, 1972. The conference, sponsored by the Young Socialist Alliance, was attended by 1,150 people.

In her book, *Woman's Estate,* Juliet Mitchell, the British women's liberation activist and author, puts forward the thesis that "If socialism is to regain its status as *the* revolutionary politics . . . it has to make good its practical sins of commission against women and its huge sin of omission—the absence of an adequate place for them in its theory."

In this she is echoing an opinion that is far from original. Everyone who is active in the women's liberation struggle or familiar with the literature of the movement has heard the same arguments in one form or another. Often we hear the charges: "The Marxist movement has always ignored the problem of women's liberation." "The socialist movement played no significant role in the struggle for women's suffrage, which proves you don't really care about women." Or, "Historically, Marxism hasn't recognized the oppression of women as a sex. It is only concerned with the oppression of women as workers."

We have heard such charges repeated so often, either from ignorance or ill will, that sometimes, even unconsciously, we begin to accept the fraudulent version of Marxism and the history of women's struggles that has been concocted to buttress such assertions. The purpose of this talk is to begin to cut through the lies in order to restore the true history of Marxism and women's liberation.

As the new stage of the struggle for women's liberation began to unfold in the late 1960s, the Marxist movement in this country—the Socialist Workers Party and the Young Socialist Alliance—responded in a revolutionary fashion. We recognized the profound importance of the fact that women as women were beginning to move into action. We threw ourselves into the movement, to learn from it, to better understand it, to help lead it in an independent and fighting direction, and win the most conscious feminists to an understanding that only a socialist revolution could provide the necessary material foundations for the complete liberation of women.

At the same time, we began the process of arming ourselves theoretically. We studied the relevant Marxist classics more deeply than before and tried to apply them to the current reality. We grounded our practice and political orientation in the fundamentals of Marxism.

Now, in addition to action and theory there is a third step we must take. That is to go back and retrace the true lines of our history in order to establish the *continuity* of Marxist theory and practice.

We have a doubly difficult job, however. Not only do we have to contend with the now familiar problems of discovering the true history of women and of writing ourselves as women back into the historical record. We must also cut through the problems created by the fact that most authors who are concerned with women's history are anti-Marxist. They are not interested in discovering what role socialist women played or accurately portraying the political positions taken by revolutionary Marxists. That is a job only we can do.

Is our theory adequate?

I want to begin by stating what I consider to be the most important generalization we must draw from the record of revolutionary Marxism in relation to the struggle against the oppression of women. It is this: From the inception of the Marxist movement to today, for nearly 125 years, revolutionary Marxists have waged an unremitting struggle within the broad working-class movement in order to establish a revolutionary attitude toward the struggle for women's liberation. They have fought to place it on a sound historical and materialist basis; and to educate the entire vanguard of the working class to an understanding of the significance of the struggles by women for full equality and for liberation from the centuries-old degradation of domestic slavery.

This battle has always been one of the dividing lines between revolutionary and reformist currents within the working-class movement; between those committed to a class-struggle perspective and those following a line of class collaboration. Women's oppression and how to struggle against it has been an issue at every turning point in the history of the revolutionary movement. Our ideological and political forebears, the revolutionary Marxists, both male and female, have led the fight against all those who refused to inscribe women's liberation on the banner of socialism, or who supported it in words but refused to fight for it in practice.

This is very important. Our opponents often try to saddle us with responsibility for the positions taken, not by the revolutionaries within the working-class movement, but by the reformists—by the right wing of the pre–World War I American Socialist Party, by the Stalinists, or else by the sectarians and ultralefts who refused to recognize the complexity of the class struggle or the need to fight for democratic rights. But those tendencies do not represent *our* tradition. It is precisely against such forces that revolutionary Marxists have battled over the decades.

The first dividing line came as early as the founding of the Marxist movement itself. The *Communist Manifesto* in 1848 boldly proclaimed:

"On what foundation is the present family, the bourgeois family, based? On capital, on private gain. . . . The bourgeois sees in his wife a mere instrument of production. He hears that the instruments of production are to be exploited in common, and, naturally, can come to no other conclusion than that the lot of being common to all will likewise fall to the women.

"He has not even a suspicion that the real point aimed at is to do away with the status of women as mere instruments of production."

The line of division established here and in all the subsequent writings of Marx and Engels on this subject was that between utopian and scientific socialism. The pre-Marxian utopian socialists—such as Fourier and Owen—were also fervent champions of the emancipation of women. But their socialism, as well as their theories on the family and women, rested on moral principles and abstract desires—not on an understanding of the laws of history and the class struggle rooted in the growth of humanity's productive capacities. Marxism for the first time provided a scientific materialist foundation, not only for socialism but also for women's liberation. It laid bare the roots of women's oppression, its relationship to a system of production based on private property and a society divided between a class that owned the wealth and a class that produced it. Marxism explained the *role* of the family within class society, and the *function* of the family in perpetuating the oppression of women.

More than that, Marxism pointed out the road to achieving women's liberation. It explained how the abolition of private property would provide a material basis for transferring to society as a whole all those onerous social responsibilities today borne by the individual family—the care of the old and sick; the feeding, clothing, and educating of the young. Relieved of these burdens, Marx pointed out, the masses of women would be able to break the bonds of domestic servitude, they would be able to exercise their full capacities as creative and productive—not just reproductive—members of society. Freed from the economic compulsion on which it necessarily rests, the bourgeois family would disappear. Human relationships themselves would be transformed into free relations of free people.

And finally, Marxism took socialism and women's liberation out of the sphere of utopian yearning by proving that capitalism itself produces a force—the working class—strong enough to destroy it, capable of carrying through the momentous task of abolishing the tyranny of the possessing few over the overwhelming majority of humankind. For the first time, socialists could stop wishing for the new and better society and begin to organize to bring it about.

The struggle for women's liberation was thus lifted out of the realm of the personal, the "impossible dream," and unbreakably linked to the victory of the progressive forces of our epoch. It became a social task in the interests of all humanity. Thus, Marxism provided a materialist analysis and a scientific perspective for women's liberation.

Those women like Juliet Mitchell who charge that Marxism does not have an adequate place in its theory for women are being dishonest. It is not the degree of adequacy in Marxism's theory that they really question. They fundamentally disagree with its materialist analysis of women's oppression and all that flows from it, including the need for a revolutionary Marxist party to lead the working class and its allies to power.

Record of the First and Second Internationals

When the First International was founded by Marx and Engels in 1864, socialist theory was put into large-scale organizational practice for the first time. In a radical departure from the laws and customs of the time, the International Workingmen's Association elected a British *woman* trade-union organizer, Henrietta Law, to its General Council. How far in advance this step was from the practice of other political organizations of the day can be judged from the fact that Marx tells of receiving letters asking if women would even be allowed to join the International. Marx himself made a motion in the General Council that special working women's branches be organized in factories, industries, and cities where there were large concentrations of women workers, adding that this should in no way cut across the building of mixed branches as well.

A year after the founding of the First International a fight erupted within the German socialist movement between the Marxists and non-Marxists. In the decades ahead the German working class would create the largest, strongest, and most influential socialist party in the pre–World War I era. But from 1865 until well into the 1880s the movement was divided between the followers of the late Ferdinand Lassalle on one hand and the Marxists under the leadership of Wilhelm Liebknecht and August Bebel on the other. In 1875 the two groups united in a single party, the SPD (Sozialdemokratische Partei Deutschlands—Social Democratic Party of Germany), but maintained sharp differences within the organization. A perspective for women's liberation was one question that divided them. The Lassalleans were opposed to demanding equal rights for women as part of the party's program. They believed that women were inferior creatures whose preordained place was in the home and that the victory of socialism would return them to their natural habitat by assuring the husband an adequate wage to provide for his entire family. Thus women would not be forced to work for a wage.

The early programs of the German Social Democrats demanded only "full political rights for adults"—leaving purposely ambiguous the question of whether or not women were considered adults. It was not until the class-struggle left wing succeeded in passing a basically Marxist program in 1891 that the party demanded political rights for all, regardless of sex, and the abolition of every law which discriminated against women in any way.

A decisive element in the victory of the Marxists on this question was the book by August Bebel entitled *Woman and Socialism,* published in 1883. Although it came out a year before Engels's *Origin of the Family, Private Property and the State,* it is basically a development of the ideas outlined by Engels, a powerful explanation of the roots of women's oppression, the forms it has taken over the centuries, the historically progressive effect of the integration of women into industrial production, and the need for a socialist revolution to clear the way for women's liberation. *Woman and Socialism* created a sensation not only in Germany but throughout Europe and was instrumental in the education of several generations of Marxists.

The adoption of a Marxist program, however, was not the end of the struggle within the SPD for a revolutionary position on women's oppression. After the Lassalleans had ceased to exist as a distinct tendency, a new reformist current arose in the party pressing for adaptation to the capitalist status quo on a variety of fronts. Clara Zetkin, one of the staunchest supporters of the Marxist left wing, led the socialist women's movement throughout the entire prewar period and fought within the SPD to develop a revolutionary perspective on the struggle for women's emancipation. Nor was Zetkin's leadership limited to this one question. In 1914, when the majority of the SPD leaders capitulated to German imperialism and voted to support their "own" ruling class in the First World War, Clara Zetkin was one of the tiny handful of German Social Democrats along with Rosa Luxemburg and Karl Liebknecht, who broke with the SPD and maintained a revolutionary internationalist position.

Throughout the early 1890s the SPD concentrated primarily on the trade-union organization of women and made some important gains. Then, in 1896, under Zetkin's urging, the SPD adopted a motion to begin developing special organizations for more extensive political activity among women. In addition to working for the general aims of the party, they were to concentrate on a whole range of issues of special concern to women: political equality, insurance for childbirth, protective legislation for women workers, education and security for children, and political education for women.

Until 1908 it was illegal for women in most of Germany even to join a political group of any kind. The SPD got around this by setting up dozens of "societies for the self-education of women workers," loose associations which were partly outside the boundaries of the party but closely linked to it. From 1900 on, biannual Socialist Women's conferences were held to unite these groups and provide leadership for them.

But the reason for these special working women's organizations was not just to solve the legal problem. Revolutionary leaders of the women's movement in Germany argued for the need to have separate women's organizations on the basis of the special needs of women, their isolation within the family, their fear of speaking out with men around, and the need to develop the leadership capacities of women.

After 1908, women were legally able to join the SPD directly and those in the special SPD women's organizations did. But the women continued to maintain their own newspaper, *Gleichheit* (Equality), edited by Clara Zetkin, which reached a circulation of more than 100,000 by 1912.

They also functioned in a somewhat special way within the SPD. For example, after 1908 women received proportional representation on all the standing committees of the party, and the women members of the committees were elected by meetings of the women comrades. This is interesting, not as a final organizational model, but as an attempt by the SPD to work out difficult problems posed by the need for both independent women's organizations and a single revolutionary party of the working class within which there are no second-class citizens and all members have equal rights and responsibilities.

With sixty or seventy additional years of revolutionary experience behind us, and the examples of the Second and Third Internationals to draw on, revolutionary Marxists have worked out different, and better, solutions to these same problems. There is no separate women's section or caucus within the SWP or YSA. Everyone has equal voice and vote in reaching all decisions on all questions. At the same time, we have special subgroups—we call them "fractions"—to organize and carry out the decisions once they are made and to help lead and direct the work. The Bolsheviks, who had to solve the same problem, likewise drew on these experiences of the German Social Democrats before them and developed an organizational form on which ours is basically modeled.

We should take note of two important points here. First is the realization that questions such as the relationship between a revolutionary party and an independent women's movement and how the leadership of this work within the party should be organized are not new problems that suddenly emerged in 1970. The Marxist movement does have a history and tradition on these questions that is worth studying and learning from.

Second is a word of warning. When we start to look into a historical question like the oppression of women and the struggle against it we need to guard against the gravest error of all—one that most of our critics in the women's liberation movement make. That is the error of approaching history in an ahistorical way. We must resist the inclination to project backward in time our current level of consciousness or stage of development instead of judging the past by what was known and what was possible then. Unless we take pains at each step to place things in their concrete historical context and understand them in that light, we will not be able to learn from the past.

I want to give three more historical examples of the way in which the question of women's liberation has been an integral part of the struggle to build a revolutionary party of the working class: first, from the early years of the American Socialist Party; second, from the early years of the Third International; and lastly, from the founding of the Fourth International.

The American Socialist Party

The backward, reactionary, patriarchal ideas concerning women's nature which were prevalent in late nineteenth-century society found their reflections within the American socialist movement, just as they did in Germany. That is to be expected. No organization is immune to pressures from the society that surrounds it. But it was the right wing of the socialist movement that acted as the main conduit for sexist ideas. Many in the left wing of the movement fought to establish a correct line in theory and in practice.

For example, it was Daniel DeLeon, the central leader of the Socialist Labor Party and one of the founders of the IWW, the Industrial Workers of the World, who translated Bebel's work, *Woman and Socialism,* for the American public. It was published in this country for the first time in 1904.

Within the Socialist Party, which was founded in 1901, quite discernible right, center, and left wings rapidly materialized. Typical of the attitude held by right-wing elements within the party was an article printed in the April 28, 1901, issue of *The Worker,* one of the many newspapers published unofficially by SP members (the SP had no official press; all its publications were individually owned and controlled and reflected differing points of view). *The Worker* explained that capitalism was forcing women to work because men earned so little. While socialists had no intention of trying to restrict women to the home, once the economic compulsion to work was removed, it was clear that "ninety-nine women out of every hundred would choose the lot of wife and mother."

A widespread attitude within the Socialist Party was similar to the then prevalent view of the Black struggle: women's oppression, like racial oppression, would be solved in passing by the class struggle. It was not a special struggle that had its own dynamic or needed its own organizational forms or put forward its own demands.

James P. Cannon, in his study, *The First Ten Years of American Communism,* describes the left wing of the Socialist Party as a "theoretically uncertain and somewhat heterogeneous minority." It took the Bolshevik revolution and the influence of the ideas and example of Lenin, Trotsky, and the new Third (Communist) International to place this left wing on solid foundations. The young Communist Party of the 1920s brought the American socialist movement out of what Cannon calls the "theoretical wasteland of its prehistory." Cannon explains at length how this help from the Comintern was decisive in educating the young Communist Party on the importance and character of the Black struggle, of convincing the party that Blacks were exploited as Blacks in addition to being exploited as workers, that a program of special demands for this oppressed nationality was needed.

I am sure a similar process took place on the question of women's oppression, as the resolutions of the early years of the Comintern on the organization of work directed specifically to women were far superior to anything the prewar Socialist Party had ever adopted.

However, the question was handled differently than the Black struggle. In the first place, there were several thousand women members of the Socialist Party as compared to a small handful of Black members. And second, the prewar and immediate postwar years saw a massive upsurge in the suffrage struggle, an actual movement involving tens of thousands of women in actions all over the country. These two features produced a real debate within the Socialist Party, and an articulate group of women and men who made their views known and tried to win the Socialist Party to a revolutionary position on feminism, on the importance of the suffrage struggle, and on other demands being raised by women.

I will return a little later to the question of the suffrage struggle, but here I want to give one example of this debate and the views put forward by some of the left-wing members of the American SP.

The *New Review,* a monthly magazine published by SP members, was one of the organs expressing the opinions of the left wing. It frequently carried articles dealing with socialism and feminism. One of the most interesting exchanges occurred in

1914, starting with the March issue. Mary White Ovington (who was also one of the founders of the NAACP) published an article entitled "Socialism and the Feminist Movement." She began by stating that "Socialism and Feminism are the two greatest movements of to-day. The one aims to abolish poverty, the other to destroy servitude among women."

She went on to explain why women were not willing to wait for socialism to begin to struggle for their rights, any more than men were; why this was a revolutionary struggle; and why the Socialist Party should pay more attention to it.

Ovington's defense of the feminist movement elicited a reply, in the May issue of the *New Review,* from British "socialist" E. Belfort Bax who informed her how ignorant she was because he, E. Belfort Bax, had conclusively proved in his book, *The Fraud of Feminism,* that things such as masculine despotism and female "slavery" did not exist. On the contrary the real problem was that of female privilege, of "woman's immunity from punishment for crimes committed against men."

Bax asserted that it was unfortunate a plank in favor of female suffrage had been included in the party's program, but it was not too late to put an end to such foolishness if people would only think rationally. "Given an average intellectual, and, in certain aspects, moral inferiority of woman as against man . . . there is obvious reason for refusing to concede to woman the right to exercise, let us say, administrative and legislative functions such as have hitherto accrued to men."

Bax's bigoted and pompous opinions brought forth an indignant response. For the rest of the year, month after month, the *New Review* carried articles blasting him. In defense of the term "feminism" one author explained:

"No one doubts that women are changing. We need an appropriate word which will register this fact. The term feminism has been foisted upon us. It will do as well as any other word. . . . It means woman's struggle for freedom." In addition to demands for changes in laws and institutions, the author developed the theme that feminism "means a changed psychology, the creation of a new consciousness in women."

Louise W. Kneeland wrote in the August 1914 issue:

"The Socialist who is not a Feminist lacks breadth. The Feminist who is not a Socialist is lacking in strategy. To the narrow-minded Socialist who says: 'Socialism is a working-class movement for the freedom of the working class, with woman as woman we have nothing to do,' the far-sighted Feminist will reply: 'The Socialist movement is the only means whereby woman as woman can obtain real freedom. Therefore I must work for it.'"

Another contribution argued that if women won the right to vote one of the things they must do is "repeal the law which, by penalizing the spread of information in regard to the prevention of conception, attempts to enforce upon women the tyranny of accidental and unwelcome pregnancy." The author added:

"There is certainly no kind of freedom where there is no command over one's own body. If a woman may not keep her body for her own uses as long as she wishes . . . she is certainly a slave."

And so it went, article after article explaining socialism and feminism in terms that sound like they could have been written in the 1970s. Reading such contributions, one senses the depth and breadth of the female radicalization at the beginning of the century, and realizes that there were many socialist women who understood the full significance of that radicalization, identified with it, and participated in it. The fact that they were not able to educate the entire socialist movement to the same level of understanding is attributable to three factors: Social prejudices against women were even deeper and more pervasive than today; American socialism was still in its "theoretical prehistory"; and the majority of the members of the Socialist Party were socialist reformers, not revolutionary Marxists.

Before going on to the early years of the Third International, I want to mention one more aspect of our revolutionary heritage in this country: the Industrial Workers of the World. When most of us think about the heroic battles of the Wobblies, their great free speech fights and strike battles, we don't visualize women as well as men. But one of the most dynamic revolutionary figures of the early years of the century, Elizabeth Gurley Flynn, was a Wobbly organizer for some ten years. She helped lead the famous Spokane, Washington, free speech fight—despite the fact that she was visibly pregnant and, according to the customs of the time, should not even have been seen in public. She played a role in the important IWW–led Lawrence textile strike in 1912 and many others. Both the IWW and the Socialist Party helped lead the hard-fought battles to unionize the textile mills and the garment industry which often employed predominantly female, immigrant labor. Socialist Party leaders and labor organizers like Rose Pastor Stokes, Ella Reeve Bloor, and Mother Jones were women who made historic contributions to American labor and socialist history.

Lenin's views on female emancipation

The Third International was built on the shoulders of the victorious Bolshevik revolution. It was founded when a line of blood was being drawn between the new revolutionary international and the old Social Democracy. No quarter was given to those who wavered between the two. It was a life-and-death struggle for the young Soviet Republic, which was fighting the invading armies of fourteen countries, trying to hold power despite the devastation of war and civil war, famine and disease, in the most economically backward country of Europe.

From 1917 through 1923, the Bolsheviks and many others saw that the struggle for state power was on the agenda not only in Russia but in Germany and other European countries as well. In this they were not wrong. But no leadership other than the Bolsheviks proved capable of meeting the challenge and grasping the historical opportunity to bring the insurgent working masses to the conquest of power.

As the first revolutionary wave subsided, many in the young international failed to understand the meaning of the new situation, the need to readjust the tactics and strategy of the international to accord with the new objective situation, the need to adopt a united-front strategy toward the Social Democracy and other working-class parties. They didn't understand that repeated denunciations of the betrayals by Social Democracy would not by themselves convince those workers still loyal to the Second International. It was necessary to expose the reformist leaders in action.

Lenin and Trotsky together led the fight in the Third International against the ultraleft tendencies that sprang up. They recognized that ultraleftist errors could be just as disastrous for a revolutionary party as reformist ones.

It is in this general political context that Lenin's opinions about the proposed work of the International Women's Commission of the Comintern should be seen. Again, this was at a new turning point in the history of the revolutionary Marxist movement. Again, analysis of women's oppression and the struggle against it figured in the divisions. However, unlike some of the earlier debates and differences, this time many of the opponents of revolutionary Marxism were ultraleft, not reformist.

Clara Zetkin's book, *Recollections of Lenin*, contains the fullest presentation of Lenin's views at this stage. Zetkin's account is based on two meetings with Lenin in Moscow in 1920. These were preliminary discussions, part of the process of drafting the resolution on work among women for the Third Congress of the Comintern in 1921.

First, Lenin urged that the document should stress "the unbreakable connection between woman's human and social position and the private ownership of the means of production." To change the age-old conditions that subjugate women within the family, communists should seek to link the women's movement with "the proletarian class struggle and the revolution." (Clara Zetkin's book is not available in English. Her report of these interviews with Lenin is included in the pamphlet *Lenin On the Emancipation of Women* [Moscow: Progress Publishers, 1968].)

Lenin next took up the organizational questions I referred to earlier. "We derive our organisational ideas from our ideological conceptions," he told Zetkin. "We want no separate organisations of communist women! She who is a Communist belongs as a member to the Party, just as he who is a Communist They have the same rights and duties."

"However," he continued, "we must not shut our eyes to the facts. The Party must have organs— working groups, commissions, committees, sections or whatever else they may be called—with the specific purpose of rousing the broad masses of women. . . ."

Zetkin commented that many party members had been denouncing her for making similar proposals on the basis that such ideas were a return to Social Democratic traditions, and that "since the Communist Parties gave equality to women they should, consequently, carry on work without differentiation among all the working people in general."

"How," Lenin asked Zetkin, "do such guardians of the 'purity of principles' cope with the historical necessities of our revolutionary policy? All their talk collapses in the face of the inexorable necessities."

"Why are there nowhere as many women in the Party as men," he demanded, "not even in Soviet Russia? Why is the number of women in the trade unions so small?" In sharp terms he defended the need to put forward special demands for the benefit of all women, of working women and peasant women, and even women of the propertied classes who also suffer under bourgeois society.

Finally, Lenin was sharply critical of the national sections of the Comintern for not doing as much as they should. "They adopt a passive, wait-and-see attitude when it comes to creating a mass movement of working women under communist leadership." He attributed the weakness of women's work in the International to the persistence of male chauvinist ideas which led to an underestimation of the vital importance of building a mass women's movement. For this reason he thought the resolution for the Third World Congress of the Comintern was especially important. The fact that it was on the agenda would itself give an impetus to the work of the sections.

Zetkin's second discussion with Lenin conveys an even richer idea of how he (and Zetkin) approached the problem of winning the masses of women on a world scale. It underscored the Bolsheviks' lack of sectarianism or ultraleftism. Their discussion makes clearer than most formal resolutions exactly how they carried out their work.

Zetkin proposed that the communist women from various countries should take the initiative in calling and organizing an international congress of women to help promote the tremendous new ferment and radicalization of women of all classes and sections of society in the post–World War I period. She suggested that they contact ". . . the leaders of the organised female workers in each country, the proletarian political women's movement, bourgeois women's organisations of every trend and description, and finally the prominent female physicians, teachers, writers, etc., and to form national nonpartisan preparatory committees."

The conference, she proposed, should take up questions like the right of women to engage in trades and professions, problems of unemployment, equal pay, labor protection for women, social care for mothers, social measures to relieve housewives, and the status of women in marriage, family legislation, and legal rights. The proposal was based on similar conferences of nonparty working women being organized inside the Soviet Union at that time.

She outlined an international campaign to publicize and build such a conference, and also pointed out how it would be necessary for the communist women themselves to work together in a disciplined fashion in order to bring it off. "Needless to say, all this requires as an essential condition that women Communists work in all the committees and at the congress itself as a firm, solid body and that they act together on a lucid and unshakable plan."

Lenin's reaction was one of wholehearted approval. But he questioned whether the Communist fraction at such a congress on an international scale would be strong enough to win the leadership of the delegates, whether the bourgeois and reformist women might not be stronger. Zetkin responded that she thought it was not a great danger because the communist women would have the best program and proposals for action. And even if they did lose, it would be no disaster. Lenin agreed. "Even defeat after a stubborn struggle would be a gain," he commented.

On further reflection, Lenin pointed out that this congress of women "would foment and increase unrest, uncertainty, contradictions and conflicts in the camp of the bourgeoisie and its reformist friends. . . . The congress would add to the division and thereby weaken the forces of the counterrevolution. Every weakening of the enemy is tantamount to a strengthening of our forces."

With Lenin's backing for the proposal, Zetkin set out to convince the sections of the International of its value, but due to the sectarian opposition of the German and Bulgarian parties, the two parties with the largest women's organizations, the whole project fell through.

What will be most striking to participants in the feminist movement today is the degree to which this proposed conference parallels the general way in which the SWP and YSA have approached the need to build a broad, mass-action-oriented campaign around the abortion issue. The reason we are concentrating at this time on one specific demand out of our whole program for women's liberation is because of the objective possibilities and present level of consciousness. But the method and concept is the same—building a broad, united action front on a principled basis.

The Third International

The resolution that was adopted by the Third Congress of the Comintern in June of 1921 dealt with political and organizational aspects of the International's orientation. The "Theses on Propaganda Work Among Women" began with a concise political analysis stressing both the need for a socialist revolution to achieve women's liberation, and the necessity for the Communist parties to win the support of the masses of women if they were to lead the socialist revolution to victory. Neither could be achieved without the other. The resolution pointed out that if the Communists failed in the task of mobilizing the masses of women on the side of the revolution, the reactionary political forces would try to organize women against them.

It stated that there were no special "female" questions. By this they did not mean that there are no issues of special concern to women or special demands around which women could be mobilized—this is clear from the demands enumerated in the resolution. This statement—which appears often in the literature of the period—simply means that there is no question of concern to women that is not also a broader social question, a question of vital interest to the revolutionary movement, for which both male and female communists must fight. It was directed not against the need to raise special demands for women, but just the opposite, to explain to the more backward male and female workers that such demands cannot be dismissed as unimportant "female concerns."

The resolution also condemned bourgeois feminism. This designation referred to the section of the women's movement that believed liberation could be achieved by reforming the capitalist system. It called on women to reject that orientation. It likewise called on women to break with the Second International and with the centrists who wavered between the Second and Third Internationals and join the Comintern to fight for their liberation on a worldwide scale.

The 1921 thesis of the Comintern explained both why there could be no separate organization for women *within* the party; and on the other hand, why there *must* be special organs of the party for work among women. It made it obligatory, indeed almost a condition of membership in the Communist International, that every section must set up a women's commission structure that would function at every level of the party from the central national leadership to the branches or cells. It instructed the parties to assure that at least one comrade be put on full-time paid staff to direct this work on a national level. And it established an International Women's Secretariat to oversee the work and call regular six-month conferences of representatives from all the sections to discuss and coordinate their activity.

Finally, the resolution outlined the general propaganda and agitational tasks and some of the key demands to be raised in all three sectors of the world: in the Soviet Union, in the advanced capitalist countries, and in the Orient (that is, in the colonial countries that were most in ferment at the time). There was no nonsense such as we hear from ultralefts today who argue that women's liberation is of interest only to the relatively privileged women in the advanced nations or a question that concerns only middle-class women.

In conclusion the resolution discussed the concrete kinds of action that could help mobilize women throughout the world. These included demonstrations and strikes, public conferences involving nonparty women, classes, cadre schools, the sending of party members into factories where large numbers of women were employed, use of the party press, and so forth. The trade unions and women's professional associations were designated as the central arenas of activity.

This resolution was implemented within the International in a very uneven way, with some sections responding well, and others changing their tempo and character of work very little. One would hardly expect anything else, given the different levels of development of its sections. For example, in the United States, the fledgling CP did establish a women's commission in 1921, but I have been unable to discover anything about what it did or did not do.

At the Fourth Congress of the Comintern, held a year and a half later at the end of 1922, the main line of the 1921 resolution was reaffirmed. The congress called attention to the fact that some sections—unspecified—had not implemented the decisions of the last congress, and urged them to rectify the default. Special mention was made of the effective work among women being done by the Chinese comrades, who had organized themselves along the lines indicated at the Third Congress. The Comintern attached great importance to work among the particularly oppressed women of colonial countries. They realized that there was no possibility of transferring power to the working class in an underdeveloped country any more than in an advanced capitalist country without mobilizing women in struggle for their liberation.

Especially pertinent to this question is an article that appeared in the June 1970 issue of the *International Socialist Review* on "Women in the Chinese Revolution." It is an interview with Chen Pi-lan, today a leader of the Chinese section of the Fourth International, who was recruited to the Chinese Communist Party in 1922 after a CP leader came to her girl's boarding school and gave a speech on "Women's Position in Society." She is an outstanding example of the kind of women who were won to the Marxist movement by the correct policies of the Communist International during its revolutionary years. Chen describes how they organized the girl's school, demanding the right to cut their hair, to have coeducation, to hold discussion circles on questions such as freedom to love and freedom of marriage, in addition to participating in strikes, May Day demonstrations, and forming working women's clubs.

What emerges from this sketchy outline of the political orientation and activities of the Third International during its early years is a strikingly clear picture. And I should point out that within the framework of this talk I have not attempted to deal with the developments that were taking place within the Soviet Union itself. To do so would even further strengthen the positive points I have stressed.

The real situation was far from one of indifference or hostility to the special oppression of women. On the contrary, the Comintern recognized the crucial importance of struggles by women around every question ranging from the right to divorce, to equal pay, to abortion, to communal kitchens and laundry services. They made it mandatory that every section of the International develop a program of demands and an orientation toward winning the leadership of mass struggles by working women, and integrated this work into the perspective of the struggle for power.

Was there resistance to this line, and an unevenness in carrying it out? Yes, of course there was. Just as there was unevenness, resistance, and backwardness on every other question on which the Third International built its foundations. But the leadership of the International led, they fought to educate the International and establish the correct political line on this key question. And where it was carried out, the correctness of the orientation was proven many times over.

Were the leaders of the International perfect in their own attitudes or understanding? Did they have the consciousness of communist men and women—or were they even as aware as we are today about the depth of the social prejudices against women, and the way these are reflected in language and innumerable socially accepted stereotypes? Of course not. Feminists today reading Lenin, or the proceedings of the Comintern congresses, or any other literature of that period, will find many examples of pleasantries at the expense of women and language which we would never allow in the revolutionary movement today.

Some point to this as "proof" that the socialist movement doesn't understand the oppression of women. This is simply a dishonest subterfuge, an example of the kind of ahistorical thinking I referred to earlier. It fails to see the wood because some of the leaves are worm-eaten. It's an attempt to substitute subjective criteria for an honest evaluation of the political line advocated, adopted, and carried out by the revolutionary Marxist movement in its evolution. Judging on that basis, which is the only one that counts in the long run, we must say that *the Third International in its early years had a more advanced, revolutionary analysis of women's oppression and the road to liberation than any previous organization in world history.*

It also makes us extremely conscious of the depth of the Stalinist counterrevolution and betrayal. On the question of women's liberation—as on the national question, youth, the united front, and others—broad layers of revolutionaries are only now starting to work back to—or up to—positions that were established by the Bolsheviks some fifty years ago. Humanity has paid an incalculable price for the break in the continuity of Marxist traditions during that lost half-century.

The Fourth International

The revolutionary ideas and methods of the early Comintern did not die with the Stalinization of the International and the political counterrevolution in the Soviet Union in the late 1920s. They were carried on by the Soviet Left Opposition, and then by the International Left Opposition. They became the bedrock on which the Trotskyist Fourth International was built. Once again, as with all the earlier turning points in the history of revolutionary Marxism, the question of women's liberation was one of the differences which divided revolutionaries from nonrevolutionaries.

The years of isolation, the economic backwardness of pre–World War I Russia, the terrible devastation of imperialist war and civil war, the great human price paid by the October Revolution in its struggle for survival were too much. The revolution could not emerge unscathed. While capitalism was not restored, under Stalin's leadership the privileged bureaucracy acquired a more and more deadly stranglehold on the revolution in all spheres—foreign policy, national minorities, political freedom, economic planning, education, etc. As an integral part of this process the gains made by women following the October Revolution were reversed, one after the other. The family was replaced on its pedestal, abortions were made illegal, divorce became more and more difficult and costly, prostitution and homosexuality again became crimes punishable by imprisonment, day-care centers were closed or their hours shortened, coeducation was eventually eliminated, and more.

Again and again the Left Opposition led by Trotsky sounded the alarm against these measures and exposed what they meant, both on the ideological plane and on the level of human suffering for millions of women. In *The Revolution Betrayed* Trotsky devoted an entire chapter to the effects of the Stalinist reaction on women and the family. He explained the material reasons why the revolution was unable to provide the necessary alternatives to the family system, and why the privileged bureaucracy was compelled in its own self-interest to reinforce the family and deepen the oppression of women.

In 1938, in an article entitled "Does the Soviet Government Still Follow the Principles Adopted Twenty Years Ago?," Trotsky summarized the process by which the gains made by women after the revolution were reversed:

"The position of *woman* is the most graphic and telling indicator for evaluating a social regime and state policy. The October Revolution inscribed on its banner the emancipation of womankind and created the most progressive legislation in history on marriage and the family. This does not mean, of course, that a 'happy life' was immediately in store for the Soviet woman. Genuine emancipation of women is inconceivable without a general rise of economy and culture, without the destruction of the petty-bourgeois economic family unit, without the introduction of socialized food preparation, and education. Meanwhile, guided by its conservative instinct, the bureaucracy has taken alarm at the 'disintegration' of the family. It began singing panegyrics to the family supper and the family laundry, that is, the household slavery of woman. To cap it all the bureaucracy has restored criminal punishment for abortions, officially returning women to the status of pack animals. In complete contradiction with the ABC of Communism the ruling caste has thus restored the most reactionary and benighted nucleus of the class regime, i.e., the petty-bourgeois family." (*Writings of Leon Trotsky, 1937–38* [New York: Pathfinder Press, 1970 and 1976], p. 166–67.)

In such terms the positions of revolutionary Marxism were carried over into our heritage upon the founding of the Socialist Workers Party and the Fourth International. We can proudly and legitimately lay claim to the unbroken continuity of a 125-year struggle by the Marxist movement against women's oppression, and to establish a socialist world which alone can lay the basis for the liberation of women. Everything we do and say today is in harmony with this tradition, and a continuation of it.

The suffrage movement and 'bourgeois feminism'

I want now to deal specifically with the suffrage movement because there is probably no other single chapter in the history of women's struggles where the position and role of socialists has been so falsified, misunderstood, or distorted.

The problem is two-sided. On the one hand, the popular historians of the suffrage movement, who are mostly anti-Marxist, have had little interest in ferreting out the role of the socialist movement. One can read book after book on the suffrage campaign and not come across even a passing reference to the participation of Marxist women.

On the other hand, many sectarian or ultraleft "socialists" have taken the position that the suffrage movement was for nothing but a trivial bourgeois reform, a diversion from the real class struggle, of no concern to working-class women who did not at all benefit from winning such a nebulous democratic right under capitalism. These so-called socialists have had no interest in discussing the real record of the revolutionary parties in the fight for female suffrage either, as it would completely contradict their fanciful sectarian interpretations.

To begin with, let me take up one question that has bothered a good many who have read some of the socialist literature on the suffrage and feminist movement at the turn of the century. Over and over, the articles and resolutions denounce "bourgeois feminism," or just plain feminism, as a threat to the working-class movement. Even today, women in organizations like the International Socialists or other sectarian groups use such references to accuse the Trotskyists of breaking with the Marxist tradition of implacable opposition to bourgeois feminism.

What was the real point at issue? What is bourgeois feminism? And why was so much fire directed against it?

First let's dispose of a misunderstanding which sometimes makes communication difficult even today. It happens that the European radical movement has always used the term feminism as synonymous with opposition to a materialist analysis of women's oppression. In this usage, a feminist is someone who consciously rejects the idea that we must abolish private property if we are to achieve women's liberation. Socialism and feminism are thus mutually exclusive.

The American radical movement—as we saw even from the articles in the *New Review*—has not always used the terms in that way. For us a feminist is any woman who recognizes that women are oppressed as a sex and is willing to carry out an uncompromising struggle to end that oppression. Thus we say the most consistent feminist must be a socialist. This difference in terminology often causes confusion and misunderstandings.

The goal of the nineteenth- and early twentieth-century suffrage movement was to achieve a reform in the voting laws, to further democratize the electoral base in the existing bourgeois states. It was a continuation of the struggle to extend the franchise to the masses that began with the crest of the bourgeois-democratic revolution in the late eighteenth century. In the United States, universal white male suffrage had been achieved by the 1830s or 1840s through a series of struggles and reform laws that finally eliminated property qualifications for white males over twenty-one years old. With the post–Civil War enfranchisement of Black male adults—the formal if not real enfranchisement— only women were denied the vote.

In Europe it was different. In most countries universal male suffrage had not been won, and often the suffrage struggle was a combined one for males and females.

As with all struggles for reforms, the suffrage movement affected and involved many different layers and all classes of society. The reform was not in and of itself unacceptable to the ruling class, the bourgeoisie. Within the limits of parliamentary democracy it could be used as a device to undercut the deepening working-class radicalization and further disguise the class nature of the capitalist state. After all, if every adult has one vote, and the poor obviously outnumber the rich by millions to one, isn't the government they elect evidently subservient to the interests of the workers?

But the fight for democratic reforms is also in the interests of the working class, as Lenin explained over and over again. It is what he called the ABC of Marxism. For example, in rejecting the views of one P. Kievsky, who had argued that socialists should abstain from the fight to win for women the right of divorce on the grounds that such a reform would be meaningless under capitalism, Lenin said:

"That objection reveals complete failure to understand the relation between democracy *in general* and capitalism. The conditions that make it impossible for the oppressed classes to 'exercise' their democratic rights are not the exception under capitalism; they are typical of the system. In most cases the right of divorce will remain unrealisable under capitalism, for the oppressed sex is subjugated economically. No matter how much democracy there is under capitalism, the woman remains a 'domestic slave', a slave locked up in the bedroom, nursery, kitchen. . . .

"Only those who cannot think straight or have no knowledge of Marxism will conclude: so there is no point . . . in freedom of divorce, no point in democracy. . . . But Marxists know that democracy does *not* abolish class oppression. It only makes the class struggle more direct, wider, more open and pronounced and that is what we need. The fuller the freedom of divorce, the clearer will women see that the source of their 'domestic slavery' is capitalism, not lack of rights. The more democratic the system of government, the clearer will the workers see that the root evil is capitalism, not lack of rights. . . .

"*All* 'democracy' consists in the proclamation and realisation of 'rights' which under capitalism are realisable only to a very small degree and only relatively. But without the proclamation of these rights, without a struggle to introduce them now, immediately, without training the masses in the spirit of this struggle, socialism is *impossible*." (From "A Caricature of Marxism and Imperialist Economism," written August–October 1916. In Lenin's *Collected Works* [Moscow: Progress Publishers, 1964], Vol. 23, pp. 72–74.)

It was in that spirit that revolutionary Marxists fought unconditionally for full male and female suffrage.

It was in the quite different spirit of reforming capitalism in order to improve an already "good system" that many bourgeois and middle-class women participated in the suffrage struggle. And they took positions that reflected their upper-class, anti–working class bias—to use Marxist terminology, their bourgeois bias. Many women honestly believed that once women gained the vote they could rid capitalism of its wars, poverty, and other evils.

In England, prior to World War I, most of the suffrage movement was demanding the vote for women on "equal terms with men." This meant on the basis of property restrictions that would have disfranchised most working-class women. Revolutionists opposed this, of course. They demanded universal female and male suffrage, nothing less. Such a fundamental difference was a difference in class outlook and program, and thoroughly justified the designation of the half-way suffragists as bourgeois in their political perspective.

In both the United States and Britain, the majority of the suffragists supported their "own" bourgeois government in the first imperialist world war. All revolutionary Marxists—male and female—opposed that war, and a class line was drawn on that question as well.

Many women within the suffrage movement opposed the perspective of independent mass actions by women to win the vote and other forms of militant tactics aimed at involving large numbers of women. For us the strategy of mobilizing the masses to take control of their own destiny is a *class* question, a question of principle.

Many suffragists in the United States appealed to racist and anti-immigrant prejudices. They argued that women should have the vote to save the South from being controlled by Blacks and the North and West by foreigners.

Revolutionary Marxists condemned such positions, fought against them, and refused to be identified with them. That is no different from what we do today. Today we polemicize with "bourgeois" and "petty-bourgeois" feminists who believe that liberation can be achieved or even advanced by voting for McGovern or some other capitalist party candidate. In the same way, we direct our fire against those feminists who oppose the perspective of mobilizing masses of women and believe they can find a personal solution either by individually dropping out of the system or by making it within the system.

In the same way we polemicize with those feminists who believe that class divisions and exploitation stem from sex oppression and not vice versa. In the same way we try to win the largest possible number of fighting women to our banner because we know that only by building a mass revolutionary party can we assure the victory of the socialist revolution and gain women's liberation.

In that sense we agree 100 percent with the condemnation of "bourgeois" feminism and our fight today is simply a continuation of our forebears' fight to win the women's movement to a working-class perspective.

Having said that, it should also be added that some of the nineteenth- and early twentieth-century attacks on bourgeois feminism did not stem from such political or revolutionary considerations. There is no doubt that many reformist, pseudosocialist, and just plain backward but revolutionary-minded men and women often used the term bourgeois feminism not as a scientific political designation, but as an epithet, an easy way to cover up for their chauvinist prejudices against women. This is basically what Lenin was referring to when he told Clara Zetkin, "we must root out the old slave-owner's point of view, both in the Party and among the masses."

If we often avoid terms like "bourgeois" or "petty-bourgeois" feminism today, it is because they are not widely understood. Over the years they have been so misused in the radical movement that they usually obscure differences rather than clarify them.

The question of "bourgeois feminism" also arose in connection with the organizational relationship between the broad suffrage movement and the work done by the socialist parties.

For example, at the world congress of the Second International held in Stuttgart, Germany, in 1907, a resolution on the fight for women's suffrage was passed which said, among other things, that women workers should campaign for the franchise, not in conjunction with the bourgeois supporters of women's rights, but in conjunction with the class parties of the proletariat. In 1908 the convention of the Socialist Party in this country passed a similar resolution. What exactly did this involve? We can be sure that such resolutions were sometimes used as justifications for a sectarian abstention from the suffrage struggle, but that was not the intent of the motions.

Such statements did not mean that the socialists would refuse to collaborate, or cooperate, or work with non-socialists or anyone else. What they did mean was that revolutionaries would refuse to compromise on questions of class principle such as the attitude to imperialist war, racism, etc. They also meant that the Social Democratic parties would carry out a campaign for suffrage in their own name. We should not forget that these were mass parties, with tens of thousands or hundreds of thousands of members, leading the entire trade-union movement in country after country. And when they talked about organizing their own forces to fight, they were talking about mass participation.

If the Socialist Workers Party was strong enough today to mobilize 30,000 or 50,000 women in the streets of New York demanding abortion-law repeal under our own banner, you can be sure we would do it. This would not be a refusal to work with other forces, or to join together to mobilize 100,000 or a million under a united-front formation. But if it were feasible we would not hesitate to call such actions on our own and urge the masses of workers to join with us, not with Shirley Chisholm or Betty Friedan.

What is meant by not collaborating with bourgeois women is well explained by Bebel in his introduction to *Woman and Socialism*. He sharply attacks the idea that women from different classes cannot fight alongside one another for specific demands aimed at eliminating the oppression of *all* women. He points out:

"The class-antagonism, that in the general social movement rages between the capitalist and the working class, and which, with the ripening of conditions, grows sharper and more pronounced, turns up likewise on the surface of the Woman's Movement; and it finds its corresponding expression in the aims and tactics of those engaged in it.

"All the same, the hostile sisters have, to a far greater extent than the male population—split up as the latter is in the class struggle—a number of points of contact, on which they can, although marching separately, strike jointly. This happens on all the fields, on which the question is the equality of woman with man, within modern society." (Published in this country as *Woman Under Social-*

ism [New York: Schocken Books, 1971], p. 5.)

Bebel's formula, "marching separately, strike jointly," the classic definition of the united-front tactic, was proposed more than forty years before it became the byword of the Third International under Lenin and Trotsky.

Socialists in the suffrage struggle

Let's review the record of what the parties of the Second and Third internationals actually did to help win the suffrage struggle.

First, and not the least important, was that they established a clear line of principle on what they were fighting for. This was settled at the 1907 Stuttgart Congress of the Second International. The Austrian Social Democrats were then in the midst of a suffrage fight and they had decided that the key task was winning universal male enfranchisement. Arguing that the demand for women's suffrage might endanger the possibility of winning the vote for working men, Victor Adler and the other reformist Austrian leaders decided not to campaign for female suffrage.

Clara Zetkin and others demanded that this question be settled by the international congress. After debate the congress voted to condemn the Austrian party for sacrificing the principle of equal rights for women to what the Austrians thought would be a more expedient position vis-a-vis the male workers.

The same question came up in Belgium, where the Social Democracy was led—as in Austria—by openly reformist forces. In 1902 and again in 1918 the Social Democrats refused to demand suffrage rights for women because they believed that most women would vote for the reactionary Catholic parties. Belgian women did not win the right to vote until after World War II.

Against this background, the fight to pass a principled, revolutionary position on women's suffrage was not an insignificant question.

With a clear, principled line established, the second important thing the Social Democracy did was make the campaign for women's suffrage international in scope. This was the origin of March 8 as International Women's Day. We know from experience in the antiwar movement that organizing and building internationally coordinated actions is no small job, and we shouldn't underestimate the impact and power of the Second International's campaign on this issue.

Taking their inspiration from the mass actions for women's suffrage organized by the socialist women in the United States, the International Socialist Women's Congress in 1910 called for an international day of action demanding universal female suffrage. The unifying theme was to be: "The vote for women will unite our strength in the struggle for socialism." The response to the call was beyond all expectations.

In Germany and Austria, for example, the action was broadly built: committees were formed, publicity put out, demonstrations and meetings organized, articles prepared for the press. Special newspapers were issued the week before the day of action. *The Vote for Women* appeared in Germany and *Women's Day* in Austria.

Alexandra Kollontai, the Russian revolutionary women's leader, described the turnout for the first Women's Day in 1911 in the following way:

"Germany and Austria . . . were one seething trembling sea of women. Meetings were organised everywhere—in the small towns and even in the villages. Halls were packed so full that they had to ask workers to give up their places to the women. This was certainly the first show of militancy by the working women. Men stayed at home with the children for a change, and their wives, the captive housewives, went to meetings." (*International Women's Day* by Alexandra Kollontai [London: North London Socialist Woman, 1972], p. 2.)

In Austria, 30,000 women and men took part in the largest street demonstration. Thereafter, International Women's Day became an annual event.

In the United States, too, the Socialist Party played an important role in the final stage of the suffrage struggle, from 1907–08 on. Party conventions discussed and debated how to participate in and organize the suffrage campaign; demonstrations and meetings were organized—demonstrations called by the party itself as well as broader ones in which the socialists took part.

In 1907, the publication *The Socialist Woman* was created as one of the many SP-oriented journals. Wherever the SP had legislators they introduced suffrage bills. In 1909, women's suffrage was one of the themes of the May Day meetings and actions. And in 1908, the party selected a full-time paid organizer to direct the work on a national scale.

In at least three states the Socialist Party campaigns around the suffrage issue played an important and perhaps decisive part in the winning of the franchise: Nevada, Kansas, and the crucial 1917 battle in New York. During the height of the New York fight, the Socialist Party organized suffrage meetings somewhere in the city every single night. SP strength in both upstate New York and New York City was probably decisive in securing the narrow margin of victory.

The Socialist Party also ran many women candidates for office, which was a demonstrative step to take. For example, Kate Richards O'Hare ran for the House in Kansas in 1910, Anna A. Maley for governor of Washington in 1912, and Ella Reeve Bloor for lieutenant governor of New York in 1918.

Far from the suffrage struggle passing the Socialist Party by, as one would assume from numerous accounts, many of the most articulate and skilled women—and certainly the most politically conscious—were in the Socialist Party. The SP was a mass party with tens of thousands of members. Feminists and suffragists like Rheta Childe Dorr joined the Socialist Party when they came to realize, as Dorr explained, that "full equalization of the laws governing men and women are part of the Socialist platform in every country of the world."

A roster of women who were in the Socialist Party reads like an honor roll of the early decades of the century: Ella Reeve Bloor, Mary Mother Jones, Kate Richards O'Hare, Margaret Sanger, Helen Keller, Anna Louise Strong, Rose Pastor Stokes, Antoinette Konikow, and many more.

In fact, Ida Husted Harper, author of the *History of Woman Suffrage, 1900–1920,* testified before the House Judiciary Committee in 1912 that the Socialist Party was "the only one which declares for woman suffrage and thereby gives women an opportunity to come out and stand by it." In her opinion this explained "why there seem to be more Socialist women than Republican or Democratic." (Cited by James Weinstein in *The Decline of Socialism in America, 1912–1925* [New York: Monthly Review Press, 1967], p. 62.)

The fact that the Socialist Party fought for women's suffrage was one reason why the SP attracted more outspoken women leaders than the capitalist parties. But that was not all that was involved. The decision to join the revolutionary working-class movement represented a qualitatively higher level of consciousness concerning the problems of women's oppression and what would be necessary to achieve liberation. The women who joined the Socialist Party did so because they understood that the only key which could open the door to their liberation as a sex was the transfer of state power from the hands of the capitalist rulers to the working class.

The Bolsheviks and the suffrage movement

The party that made the greatest contribution to the struggle for women's suffrage, however, was not the amorphous American SP but the more unequivocally revolutionary Russian Bolsheviks. And their contribution was not only national but international in scope.

Despite the illegal conditions of czarist repression, both the Mensheviks and the Bolsheviks organized activities for International Women's Day starting in 1913. Alexandra Kollontai describes how they organized an illegal "Morning Teach-In on the Woman Question" in Petrograd in 1913 (at the end of which almost all the party speakers were arrested). She points out what an inspiration this action was—despite the arrests—to others around the world.

Those early actions in 1913 and 1914 laid the basis for the massive women's demonstration of March 8, 1917 (February 23 by the Russian calendar), when the Petrograd women poured into the streets demanding "Bread for our children," and "The return of our husbands from the trenches." The Russian Revolution marked its beginning from that day.

The legal equality won by the women of Soviet Russia was a tremendous embarrassment to the so-called democracies around the world where women were denied the right to vote. Women in Russia won the franchise with the February Revolution and during 1917–18 pickets at the White House frequently carried placards contrasting "Free Russia" with "Kaiser Wilson."

Supporters of the Women's Party in the U.S. started a "watch fire" in an urn in front of the White House and every time Wilson made a speech abroad that referred to freedom, even in passing, a copy of the speech was burned in the watch fire. Women around the world gained powerful support in their suffrage demands from the fact that even in "backward" Russia women had won the right to vote.

With the victory of the Bolsheviks in October, a woman assumed a cabinet post for the first time in history. Alexandra Kollontai became the head of the Social Welfare Ministry. When Kollontai was later appointed the first woman ambassador in history, the aristocratic diplomatic corps of the world was rocked by convulsions. Not only was she a woman, but a "morally loose" one at that, who was hardly fit to associate with kings, queens, and heads of state.

We can point to the victory of the Russian Revolution and the establishment of the first workers' state in the world as an historic contribution by our forebears to the struggle for women's suffrage, women's liberation, and the progress of all humanity.

What I have tried to do in this talk should be seen as a beginning. Much more research needs to be done. As we unearth new material, discover new sources, and establish new facts, new conclusions will inevitably suggest themselves. We may want to modify, adjust, or further develop our initial impressions and evaluations. But this is the beginning of the process of retying the threads of continuity in our Marxist history and renewing our traditions. The deeper we go in this process of rediscovering our own past, the richer will be our understanding of today, the better prepared and more confident we will be to break new ground as we face new tasks and challenges in the future.

TOWARD A MASS FEMINIST MOVEMENT
Resolution adopted by the SWP National Convention, August 1971

The new feminism

Few myths are on the surface so irrational, yet at the same time so widely believed, as that of the inferiority of women. For thousands of years, people all over the world have been taught to believe that women are biologically and intellectually inferior to men, with an emotional constitution that makes their acceptance of a subservient role in society natural.

Throughout history, women have rebelled against this, and fought for improvements in their status. But never before has there been a feminist movement as irreconcilable in its opposition to oppression, as radical in its critique of the social forces that breed these inequities, and as potentially powerful a force for helping to end that oppression, as the emerging movement of today.

The most outstanding characteristic of this new movement is its deep-going challenge of every aspect of the oppression of women, including the hitherto unquestioned "sacred" role of women in the family. The fundamental proposition being put forward by feminists today is that it is not biology but social institutions which have kept women "in their place" in the home; that the present-day psychological difference between men and women—and even to some extent their physical differences—have been culturally conditioned, not biologically determined.

This bold denial of biological inferiority is part of the unprecedented militancy of feminism today. For the first time in history, large numbers of people are beginning to grasp the depth of women's oppression, the degree to which womankind has been systematically stunted, warped and dehumanized to fit the role of wife-mother-housekeeper.

At the heart of this radicalization of women is the growing contradiction between the tremendous wealth of American society, the fact that the material resources already exist to free women from domestic slavery, and the reality that this is not being done by the capitalist social order. For the first time in history, large numbers of women are becoming conscious that there are alternatives to their present roles.

The consciousness that *society* is responsible for women's second class status is reflected in all aspects of the feminist movement's activities. It can be seen in the consciousness-raising groups, where women discuss how their personal problems are not the result of their own individual failings, but flow from a basic oppression suffered by all women. It is expressed repeatedly in feminist literature. Most importantly, it can be seen in the *actions* of masses of women in which demands have been raised for free 24-hour child care centers, free abortions on demand, and equal job and educational opportunities. If realized, such measures would bring much closer the day when women can make a choice about what they want to do with their lives.

Since the beginning of class society and the emergence of the patriarchal family system women of all classes have been relegated to the confines of the home and assigned the social responsibility of child-raising and housekeeping. Women have never consciously chosen this role, but have been trained from birth to feel that their fulfillment can come only from marriage and child-rearing. Even when women have been forced, or have chosen to take jobs outside the home, they have been charged with neglecting their "first responsibility" to the family. Thus, women have been prevented from being independent human beings. They have been dependent, both for economic security and for their very psychological identity and estimate of self-worth, on their husbands, fathers or boyfriends.

The role of women in the family means that the birth of a child commits a woman to years of work and drudgery. Because women lack complete control over the decision to have children, they lack control over their own lives. The vulnerability and dependency which flows from this is an important aspect of every woman's existence. It helps to reinforce the concept that women are basically powerless.

Changes in the family and the roots of the new movement

Since its emergence at the dawn of civilization, the family institution has evolved and changed according to the different class structures and needs of the systems of slavery, feudalism, and capitalism.

The industrial revolution was a key turning point in this evolution. Industrialization progressively displaces earlier forms of production centered around the family where goods were produced on the family farm or estate or in the family shop or small business, and much of what each individual family consumed in the way of clothes and food was produced by the family members. The role of women in the family economic unit clearly defined their role in society. Women had little identity aside from their functions within the family, and even fewer rights. They could not travel, speak in public, engage in politics, go to college, drink in the taverns or mix in society at large in any significant way.

Industrialization began to lay the basis for the replacement of the family by creating the possibility of relieving women of their economic functions in the home, and by giving them an independent productive role outside the home. As mass production developed, for the first time in thousands of years, women were drawn away from the family to outside work. Brutal and exploitative though it was, industrialization, by bringing women out of the home, led to a more and more obvious contradiction between the restrictions put on women in public activities and the need for them to participate in industry.

The rapid industrialization and urbanization of American society were key factors which led to the rise of the women's rights movement in the 19th and early 20th centuries. It was part of and a sequel to a general worldwide upsurge in the period of the bourgeois-democratic revolutions against the traditional, inherited privileges of the ruling class under feudalism. In the United States, it grew out of the radicalization preceding the Civil War and got much of its impetus from the abolition movement.

At the first Women's Rights Convention in 1848 in Seneca Falls, New York, a Declaration of Sentiments was passed, which called for women to have "immediate admission to all the rights and privileges which belong to them as citizens of the United States." Specifically this included the right to vote, property rights, freedom from the domination of the husband, the right to have a profession, to go to college, to better wages, and an end to the moral double standard between men and women.

The new rise of the American feminist movement is as much a response to the era of capitalism in its death agony, as the earlier women's movement was a response to the social conditions created by 19th century capitalism.

The demands of the present movement go beyond those of the earlier women's rights movement, while at the same time building upon the aims and achievements of this earlier struggle. The feminist movement today is still demanding equality—in pay, in opportunity, in the types of options women have in life—but there is a much more radical understanding that real equality cannot be won without the full right of women to control their bodies, without economic independence and without social alternatives to private responsibility for the raising of children within the individual family.

Whereas the early women's movement spoke in terms of gaining equal rights within American capitalist society, the feminist movement of today started out by questioning the basic structure and institutions of this society, especially the family. This new level is reflected in the demands raised at the Congress to Unite Women, held in November 1969 in New York City, one of the first major conferences of the women's liberation movement. It outlined some of the basic goals of fundamental importance to all women that are being raised by the feminist movement: 24-hour child care centers open to all children from infancy to early adolescence regardless of their parents' income or marital status, with child care practices being decided by those using the centers; free abortion on demand, no forced sterilizations—the right of women to control their own bodies; equal job opportunities; an end to the tracking system in education; women's studies programs; enforcement of Title VII of the 1964 Civil Rights Act which calls for equality on the job; an end to the derogatory image of women presented by the media; and passage of the Equal Rights Amendment.

The early women's rights movement disintegrated after 1920, creating a 50-year hiatus during which economic and social changes in the U.S. laid the basis for the emergence of the new feminist movement and the more radical demands of today. The giant expansion of technology and industrialization, which has accelerated since World War II, has removed productive activities from the family to an unprecedented degree. The old family farm has virtually disappeared. Modern appliances, frozen and packaged foods, and ready-made clothes are all examples of the degree to which productive activities have been transferred out of the individual, isolated family unit, to be carried out on a mass production basis.

The role of women is directly affected by these changes in the nature of the family which have narrowed the tasks of millions of housewives to such functions as care of the very young and very old, and janitorial and cooking tasks around the house. Along with this is the fact that the average American woman has fewer children. For tens of millions of women this has meant that for the greatest period of her life, her domestic role consists only of caring for her own and her husband's personal needs.

At the same time, more women than ever before are working outside the home, and those who do, continue to be discriminated against on the job. More than 43 percent of all adult American women are today employed outside their own homes. This represents a major increase from 1960 when the figure was 37 percent, and from 1950, when it was 34. And the percentage continues to increase. Women earn, on the average, 40 percent less than employed males, and the gap between the wages of men and women is widening, not narrowing. The best paying jobs, almost without exception are closed to women.

In addition, women continue to have a double burden—their jobs and their "duties" at home. For working women with children, facing a situation where there are few child care facilities available, this double burden is especially oppressive.

More women than ever before in history are receiving more and more education. Between 1950 and 1966 the percentage of American women aged 20–34 attending schools quadrupled. In the last decade, the number of white women with at least four years of high school climbed from 65 to 80 percent. Among Black women, the figure went from 40 to 61 percent. Hundreds of thousands of women enter the country's colleges and universities every year. The number of women with some college education rose 160 percent in the last decade, against a 100 percent rise for men. Yet the gap continues to widen on all levels between the education and training women receive, and the availability of job opportunities commensurate with their skills. Even a superior education does not qualify women for most jobs held by less educated men.

Finally, the contradiction continues to deepen between the scientific and technological potential women see for emancipating themselves from the home and gaining control over their lives and bodies, and the fact they are denied this liberation. Technology and resources remain under the control of the ruling class who would destroy humanity; while child care centers, hospitals, schools and food centers are not built, and reactionary abortion laws, forced sterilization schemes, and a lack of adequate education about and safe methods of birth control deny women the right to control their lives.

Thus while women see the increased potential to free themselves from domestic servitude, escape the crushing burdens of poverty, and participate fully in the activities of society, they are denied this opportunity. They are told that, unlike men, their identity and worth still come from the degree of their success in finding a husband, settling down in a home, and having children. Just when millions of women see more material possibility than ever to develop, more options than ever before about what they can do with their lives, more reason than ever to believe in their own intelligence and abilities, they remain strait-jacketed by the basic wife-mother-housekeeper role assigned to females. The thoroughgoing radicalism of the new feminist movement is partly a product of these growing contradictions.

The new feminism is also a product of the broader radicalization taking place in this country, just as the women's rights movement of the l9th century was an outgrowth of the abolition struggle of that time. The civil rights movement, the ghetto rebellions, the student struggles, and the massive mobilizations against the Vietnam war, and the changing moods and struggle attitudes of young workers, have all helped to create a political climate conducive to women beginning to question their role in society. And many of the initiators of the women's liberation movement began to organize around their own oppression as a result of their experiences in other sections of the mass movement.

Of special importance in sparking the feminist movement was the nationalist radicalization of Black people and other oppressed nationalities who are rebelling against the myths of supposed biological inferiority which have been used to keep them "in their place." The assertion of Black pride and Black power, in particular, helped spark the explosion of feminist consciousness, pride and sisterhood which have been necessary to the growth of the feminist movement.

The function of the family

There is no institution in class society whose true role is as hidden by prejudices and mystification as that of the family. Much religious teaching is devoted to reinforcing the monogamous family unit, any deviation from which is labelled as "sin." The bourgeois scholars of all disciplines have been united in rationalizing the existence of the nuclear family and the oppression of women. Bourgeois psychology has upheld the basic definition of women as dependent and submissive, and has labeled any initiative or aggressiveness on the part of women as "unnatural." Bourgeois historians have hidden the true history of the struggle of women and have portrayed women activists and political leaders in a way calculated to make it difficult to identify with them. Bourgeois sociologists uphold the subordination of women in the family.

Bourgeois anthropologists perpetrate the myth that the family economic unit has always existed, and that women have always been subservient to men and played a limited social role because of their childbearing. They deny the fact that the origin of the patriarchal family coincided with, and flowed from, the development of private property, class society and the state. They hide the fact that in early communal societies, the basic *economic* unit was the clan, not an individual family. Within each clan goods were shared equally, and people worked in a cooperative way rather than competing against one another.

The historic turning point in the transfer of the central economic and social functions from the clan to the family came with the development of an economic surplus and individual accumulation of this surplus as private property. Individuals began to separate themselves from the clan and set up separate households. Women became isolated from communal activity, and monogamy for the wife was strictly enforced to assure legitimate heirs.

Today, the patriarchal nuclear family unit remains as the basic economic cell of class society, and women continue to be isolated in individual households, dependent on individual men for economic survival. For working women, women in working-class family units, and women of oppressed nationalities, the role women are forced into is the most oppressive, both to themselves and their children. They are obliged to accept the worst jobs and have even less access to educational opportunities, childcare, safe abortions or birth control. This means greater economic vulnerability and dependence on a man. The alternative is often welfare. If a woman works, she may have to leave her children uncared for.

The fact that these women suffer most from their oppression as women stems from the fact that the family is one of the basic instruments through which the social and economic inequities between different classes are perpetuated. Under capitalism, the nuclear family is assigned the responsibility for providing for the welfare of its members—food, clothing, health care, child care, education and care of the old and sick. And each family is thrown into competition with all others to get a larger share of the available jobs, goods and services.

An important aspect of the class struggle under capitalism has been the fight to force the ruling class to shoulder more and more of the responsibility for social welfare. Concessions have been won in this struggle, even though all are limited in their scope. They include social security benefits, medicare, free public education through high school, welfare, unemployment insurance, and state-financed colleges. These concessions represent significant advances, but the ruling class is constantly pushing to cut back on even the small gains made, which come nowhere close to providing for basic needs.

The demands being raised by the feminist movement today represent the sharpest challenge yet to the concept that the individual family must take full economic responsibility for each of its members. Demands like free 24-hour child care for all begins to place responsibility for rearing children on society as a whole and point in the direction of a redivision of social wealth so fundamental that it begins to bring into question the whole capitalist system.

The role played by women in the household serves as the chief rationalization for the oppression of women in all other spheres. The unique "duties" of women in the family are used to justify unequal job and educational opportunity, unequal pay, the exploitation of women as sex objects, the discrimination against women in all areas including the arts, sports, scientific research, etc., and the use of women as a component of the reserve army of labor.

The family system also plays a crucial role for capitalism in inculcating the norms and values of the private property system. The 19th century utopian socialist, Robert Owen, summarized this function of the family in the following way:

> The children within these dens of selfishness and hypocrisy are taught to consider their own individual family is their whole world, and that it is the duty and interest of all within that little orb to do whatever they can to promote the advantages of all the legitimate members of it. With these persons, it is *my* house, *my* wife, *my* estate, *my* children, *my* husband; *our* estate, and *our* children; or *my* brothers, *my* sisters; and *our* house and property.

Within the patriarchal family, the children receive training in submissiveness to authority, a training which is necessary to an economic system which demands acceptance of the right of the rich to rule. The family is an authoritarian structure, with the man considered the head and the women and children dependent on him. Obedience to the father and to the norms of the monogamous family unit helps to prepare the child for acceptance of the ideology of class society. The fostering of a child's loyalty to the individual family unit is paralleled by the inculcation of patriotism and chauvinism. The family plays the central role in implanting in infants and children the character structure without which no one could accept the hierarchical, exploitative, and alienating social relations intrinsic to capitalism.

The opponents of the women's liberation movement maintain that the feminist opposition to the family system is a challenge to the existence of affectionate relationships between people. But in reality, the family system and class society are the real destroyers of genuine human relationships.

Until the bourgeois revolution, among the wealthy and powerful possessing classes, the choice of a husband or wife was made strictly on the grounds of economic considerations, usually by the parents of the couple. It was only with the rise of capitalism, with its concept of free exchange and free labor, that the idea of freedom of choice of marriage partners evolved along with other democratic ideas. However, despite this assertion that relationships between husband and wife should be based on free choice and affection, the old economic basis of the marriage tie remained, and along with it, the institutions of adultery and prostitution.

The fact that people are free to choose their own partners in marriage does not bring freedom and happiness within marriage any more than "freedom" to sell one's labor power means that a worker is truly free. So long as women and children are dependent on the male for their economic existence and psychological identity, they will tend to be subordinate to him in their personal relationships. This means that millions of people who do not want to live together, who often do not even like each other, will continue to live together, because they feel they have no other choice. When feminists oppose the patriarchal family system, they are talking about eliminating this economic compulsion, so that personal relationships will be freed from these economic fetters.

A factor which has promoted this radical critique of the family made by feminists today has been the fact that the family has come under attack as part of the general radicalization. More and more people are becoming alienated from the decadent social relationships inherent in the death agony of a society oriented toward labor exploitation, competition, and accumulation of private property. Many, especially young people, are beginning to see the hypocrisy of capitalism's reverence for the "sacred" family system. They see that while popular magazines and other media praise the ideals of family "togetherness," the relationships between human beings are distorted by the crassest marketplace ideas. Husbands and wives are chosen on the competitive sex market; the husband according to his status, the wife according to her value as a sex object. The children are seen as "products" produced by the family, with each family making "investments" in its children to prepare them for "success" in the competitive world. This get-ahead mentality is reflected not only within the family, but also in friendships since social relationships are calculated according to what would be most beneficial in the competitive struggle to survive or advance.

The capitalist system itself has been laying the basis for the disintegration of the basic economic, competitive family unit. The rising divorce rate, the number of children running away from home, the open experimentation with communes and collectives, increasing social acceptance of deviations from the sexual mores of the patriarchal family system, and the increased number of people living together without legal marriage certificates are all signs of this disintegration. The ideological covering that has hidden the true role of this institution is becoming more and more transparent.

The disintegration of the family has also been affected by other products of the continuing technological revolution and urbanization of capitalism including the increased mobility of the population, the breaking down of traditional community ties, and the decline in religion. The "sexual revolution" is a result, not primarily of the pill, but of these broader changes in people's outlook.

Capitalism produces its own grave diggers in more ways than one. The higher the level of material and technological development, the more obvious it becomes to broader and broader layers of the population that the social forms and institutions of class society have ceased to play a progressive role. On the contrary, they have become reactionary blocks to the further advancement and welfare of humanity.

In this sense, we are on the threshold of a turning point in world history similar to the turning point thousands of years ago when the private property system replaced the communal clan system. Just as the beginning of class society and private property were associated with the separation of women into individual households, so the transition to socialism will go hand in hand with the emergence of women from their dependence on individual men within the home into full participation in public life and social production.

Revolutionary strategy for the feminist movement

While the early women's rights movement, which was able to go part of the way in the struggle for liberation, was an aspect and extension of the bourgeois-democratic revolution, the current female liberation struggle—including the demands for the deferred democratic rights of equality—is part of the process of the developing anticapitalist revolution. The question of how to end the oppression of women flows from, and is tied into, the question of how to end class society. The strategy of the feminist movement must flow from a basic analysis of how capitalism perpetuates itself, and what forces must be mobilized in struggle to eliminate it.

In the United States we are facing the strongest, best organized and most conscious ruling class in history. No small or insignificant force will be capable of taking power from its hands. There are no "individual solutions" for large numbers of people. The struggle must be aimed at taking the resources away from those who control them for personal profit and placing them under the control of the vast majority.

The women's liberation movement represents the emergence of new forces which have the potential for organizing tens of millions of women in independent struggle. It is a struggle with its own unique roots, dynamic and demands. But at the same time, the fundamental questions of strategy which the movement poses are not new. They are basically the same strategic questions posed by every developing mass movement.

The building of any mass movement requires the understanding that the ruling class in this country maintains its dominance through illusion as well as violence. A key illusion among the oppressed masses that helps perpetuate class rule is the belief that the system is capable of reforming itself and satisfying the needs of the vast majority. It is only through the experience of struggle that it becomes clear to masses of people that they must take over and control society for themselves if their demands are to be fully met. And it is through struggle that the oppressed and exploited begin to see the potential power they have to do this.

A revolutionary strategy for the feminist movement must be based on a program of democratic and transitional demands, rooted in the needs of the masses of women, and part of the broader transitional program of the socialist revolution. A program of struggle around such demands will have a revolutionary logic because they mobilize masses in struggle against the ruling class and its government, and to win them in full requires a socialist revolution.

The key question facing the revolutionary socialist party, then, is how to help mobilize masses of women—around what demands and through what forms can this be done, related to the immediate needs and level of understanding of masses of women.

No full program for the women's liberation movement has yet been worked out, and it is impossible, at this time, to develop such a full program of demands. However, the broad outlines of such a program have begun to emerge and some of the key demands are already clear.

The right to control one's own body
One set of demands are those centered around the right of women to control their own bodies:
- repeal all abortion laws
- free abortion on demand, no forced sterilizations
- free, widely disseminated birth control information
- free and safe birth control devices available to all
- a crash program of government funded research adequate to develop totally safe and effective birth control and abortion methods

The right of a woman to decide for herself when and if she will have a child is a fundamental precondition to liberation. So long as a woman cannot control what goes on inside her own body, so long as she remains the victim of state-enforced motherhood, she does not have control over the most basic factors determining her life. Precisely because alternatives exist, the denial of adequate birth control and abortion are among the most brutal aspects of women's oppression. Millions of women are coming to see this with increasing clarity and to demand changes.

Freedom from domestic slavery
The necessity of freeing women from the bonds of domestic slavery and establishing social responsibility for the important social function of the care and raising of children has given rise to a series of demands:
- free, 24-hour child care centers, open to all children from infancy to early adolescence regardless of parents' income or marital status; child care practices to be decided by those who use the centers
- low-cost, high quality cafeteria and take out food services available to all
- low-cost, high quality laundry facilities available to all
- low-cost cleaning services organized on an industrial basis available to all
- a crash, government-financed development program to provide adequate housing for all; no rent to exceed 10 percent of income; no discrimination against single women or women with children

We counterpose such demands to the ultraleft concept of abolishing or destroying the family. The family cannot be "abolished" by fiat. It can only be replaced over time. Our goal is to create economic and social alternatives which are superior to the present family system and better able to provide for the needs currently met, however poorly, by the family system, so that personal relationships will be a matter of free choice and not economic compulsion.

Economic freedom

To assure full economic independence for women we demand:
- equal pay for equal work
- no discrimination against women in any job classification
- passage of the Equal Rights Amendment to the constitution and enforcement of Title VII of the 1964 Civil Rights Act, in order to guarantee an end to all discrimination against women on the basis of sex
- the extension of "protective legislation" (providing special working conditions for women) to cover men, in order to provide better working conditions for both men and women and prevent the protective legislation from being used to discriminate against women
- guaranteed jobs at union wages for all women who are able and want to work
- preferential hiring, training and upgrading of women and oppressed national minorities, coupled with a sliding scale of hours and wages to combat unemployment and inflation
- full paid maternity leaves with no loss of job or seniority
- full compensation at union rates during periods of unemployment for all women and men, including youth who cannot find a place in the work force, regardless of marital status, protected against inflation by automatic increases, adequate to provide a decent standard of living

In putting forward and fighting for these and other demands of the women's liberation movement, working women will be forming their own organizations, as well as working through the organized labor movement, insisting that the unions adopt these demands as their own. This will be an integral part of the fight to transform the unions into instruments of revolutionary struggle fighting in the interest of the working class as a whole.

Three major trade unions—the United Automobile Workers, the American Federation of Teachers and the American Newspaper Guild—have adopted convention resolutions incorporating demands of the women's liberation movement for maternity leave, child care centers and an end to discrimination against women workers. At the 1970 AFT convention, women delegates formed a caucus to fight for their demands.

A national organization of women government workers was formed in 1968—Federally Employed Women. It now has 1,000 members in 30 chapters across the country. One-half of the members are Black women. In New York City, women workers for the city government have formed Women in City Government United, which participated in the August 26, 1970 demonstration. It is fighting discrimination against women in city jobs, for abortion coverage in women workers' health insurance, and for free 24-hour child care centers.

Equal education opportunities

To combat the educational and psychological conditioning which prepares women for an inferior, second-class status, we demand:
- an end to the "tracking" system, beginning in the primary grades, which guides women towards socially acceptable courses and careers such as homemaking, secretarial skills, nursing and teaching
- open admissions for women to all institutions of higher education; special programs to encourage women to enter traditionally male-dominated fields
- women's studies programs controlled by women to teach the truth about women throughout history
- self-defense training courses open to all women
- the right of pregnant women and unmarried mothers to remain in regular educational institutions
- an end to the textbooks' and mass media's derogatory and stereotyped portrayal of women as sex objects, and stupid, weak, emotionally dependent creatures
- university facilities for and financing of child care centers and abortion-contraception services for students and employees

Because of the key role played by students and young women in the feminist movement as a whole, struggles on campuses and in the high schools can play an important part in helping to spark struggles by other women. The struggle to win control of university facilities to benefit women, such as medical facilities for abortion, and classroom and library facilities for women's studies, provides an example for the general fight to win control of the resources of society away from the ruling class and its apologists. In addition, the campuses can serve as vital organizing centers for the feminist movement to reach out to broader layers of oppressed and exploited women.

Women prisoners

To combat the special forms of legal victimization of women by the police and judicial apparatus, we demand:

- abolition of all special legal penalties for women
- abolition of all laws victimizing prostitutes
- full right to conjugal visits
- review the cases of all women prisoners by a commission of their peers; release all imprisoned or held without fair trial by their peers

Imperialist war

Because women, along with every other oppressed or exploited sector of the population, pay the price of the ruling class' imperialist aggression around the world, the women's liberation movement should demand:

- immediate and unconditional withdrawal of all U.S. troops from Vietnam
- no American troops to be sent by the imperialist government to intervene in the affairs of another country
- abolish the capitalist draft
- funds previously used for war to be used to finance free child care facilities, abortion clinics and hospitals, schools, housing, and provide guaranteed jobs at union wages

Women of oppressed nationalities

The feminist movement recognizes that most Black, Chicano, Puerto Rican, Native American and Oriental American women suffer a triple oppression—as women, as workers and as oppressed nationalities—and that their struggle will, for this reason, take different forms. Black feminism and Black nationalism, Chicano nationalism and Chicana feminism are complementary aspects of the deepening revolutionary consciousness among millions of oppressed women. The movement of oppressed nationalities and the women's liberation movement have already had a profound effect on each other.

Black feminism leads Black women to a discovery of their identity as human beings and therefore builds a new confidence and spirit of struggle against all forms of oppression that Black women face. Groups such as the Phoenix Organization of Women, a predominantly Black and Puerto Rican group of ex-drug addicts in New York, have played a vanguard role in building the women's liberation movement. Within all the various Black organizations, discussions and debates are taking place over the question of the relationship of the Black movement to the women's liberation movement. More and more women of the oppressed nationalities are coming to the conclusion that feminist ideas are deeply relevant to their lives and are organizing to fight their oppression as women as well as their national oppression.

Women's liberation demands were incorporated by La Raza Unida Party of Northern California as a part of the party's platform. The same question will be raised in connection with the rise of any independent Black political party or labor party.

The demands already discussed are of great importance to the women of oppressed nationalities precisely because it is they who suffer the most from the domestic enslavement of women and the reactionary character of the patriarchal family system. In addition to these fundamental demands of the feminist movement, women of oppressed nationalities are also fighting, as an integral part of their struggle for liberation as women and as members of oppressed nationalities—for the right of the Black, Chicano, Puerto Rican, Native American and Oriental American communities to control the institutions which affect their lives. Of key importance is the struggle for the child care facilities, abortion and medical facilities and schools to be placed under the control of boards elected by the oppressed nationalities themselves.

A perspective of mass action

Around these demands, and others like them which will emerge in the course of the struggle and the development of the feminist movement, it will be possible to build a mass women's liberation movement. However, it is not enough simply to have a correct program of demands based on the needs of women. We must also have a correct appreciation of how to mobilize large numbers of women in struggle to win their demands.

Two basic questions must be answered:

1) Given the fact that women are divided by class, race, age, and other factors, what *are* the possibilities for uniting women in the struggle for liberation?

2) What is the relationship between the feminist movement and other social movements against the oppression and exploitation of capitalism such as the antiwar movement, the movements of oppressed nationalities, the student movement and the struggles of labor?

Two main incorrect points of view have been put forward within the women's liberation movement in regard to the first question. There are some women who say that the class and racial divisions among women are unimportant. This tendency is often reflected in the attempt to designate women as "an oppressed class." Those who hold this view say that all that is needed for the liberation of humankind is a mass independent women's movement because the oppression of women is primary, other forms of oppression flow from it, and thus all other struggles derive from, or are aspects of, the feminist struggle.

At the other extreme are some women who say that the divisions among women are insurmountable and that there is no basis for uniting women in struggle except around solely working-class demands. Those who hold this viewpoint tend to deny the significance of the oppression of women as a sex and hold that the feminist struggle should be subordinated to and wait for other struggles. They denigrate the battle for democratic demands and cannot see that they are in the direct interest of the working class.

The truth is that women are at the same time both united by sexist oppression and divided by class society. There is an objective basis for a unified struggle of women of different nationalities and classes because all women are oppressed as women by capitalism. Sisterhood *is* powerful because of this universal female oppression, and this is the basis for the existence of an independent non–exclusive mass feminist movement, with an anticapitalist logic.

Women of different social classes suffer to very different degrees from lack of child care and abortion facilities, unequal pay, job discrimination, warped education and social conditioning. But these are all aspects of the very real oppression of women and all women have a stake in struggling around these issues. The broadest unity in struggle, closed to no woman, is possible and progressive if this unity is based on demands which mobilize women in struggle and which combat the oppression of women perpetuated by capitalism. Women of the working class have the most to gain by united struggles around these issues.

Because women suffer different forms and degrees of oppression, different groupings will organize separately, as well as together. Black women, and women of the other oppressed nationalities will organize as Blacks, as Chicanas, as Puerto Ricans, because they suffer a unique oppression. Working women will organize to further their struggles on the job and in the union. High school students, college students, women belonging to religious organizations, gay women, and other groups of women are all already showing a need to organize separately around the particular oppression they face. In fact this independent organization is necessary to most effectively mobilize the largest numbers of women in broad-based actions.

Any attempt to disregard either those factors which divide women or those which unite them will lead to misunderstandings and roadblocks in the attempt to mobilize the full power of women.

The answer to the second question, that is, the question of the relationship between the feminist struggle and other movements against the oppression and exploitation of capitalism, lies in the fact that the feminist movement, and the struggle against imperialist war, the liberation struggles of the oppressed nationalities, and the labor movement, must all have one goal in common if their demands are to be realized: the destruction of the capitalist system. So long as production is organized on the basis of private property and profit, so long will the material foundations which gave rise to the family and the domestic servitude of women exist—as well as war, racism, economic exploitation and alienation. Women have a basic interest in supporting and joining with others whose struggles will lead them in an anticapitalist direction.

At the same time, the feminist movement is also a struggle which is different and independent from all other movements, because it is based on a unique oppression. The movement therefore has its own dynamic and its own unique course of development. While women need allies, it is only women, organized independently on the basis of struggle against their common oppression and with a correct program of struggle who can win full female liberation. No other movement can substitute for this.

A correct program of democratic and transitional demands for the female liberation movement, an understanding of how women are united and divided, and a knowledge of how the feminist movement is related to other mass struggles points directly to the kind of strategy necessary for advancing the women's liberation movement. We want to be the best builders of the campus women's groups, Black and Chicana groups, high school groups, women's caucuses within unions and on the job, and all the other kinds of women's organizations which will grow up as women begin to struggle. We will want to be involved in and build the varied activities of such organizations—conferences, actions, publications and educational and consciousness-raising activities.

Consciousness-raising groups, and the general consciousness raising that comes from being part of a broad movement, can help give women confidence to get out of the isolation of their homes, and courage to lead independent lives and gain independent identity and strength. Small–group consciousness raising is not an end in itself, but can be a vital part of laying the basis for taking action against female oppression.

The central role of action coalitions and mass mobilizations

In addition to building all the separate components of the feminist movement our central goal is to build broad coalitions based on agreement to struggle around specific issues, like abortion or child care, and having a perspective of mobilizing broad layers of women in *action* independent of the ruling class and its political parties. Such a mass action perspective will counter tendencies to turn the movement inward through livingroom feminism and counterinstitutionism, and it will orient the movement toward reaching out and mobilizing masses of women who are ready to fight for issues that are of immediate concern for them, and by so doing, advance the struggle for complete liberation of all women. Such coalitions must be built on the basis of non-exclusion and democratic norms. They must reject lesbian-baiting and red-baiting in all its forms. They must reach out to the largest possible numbers of women, explaining the significance of the key demands being raised, and involving them in action.

The importance of building such broad, mass-action coalitions was shown clearly by the August 26, 1970 actions. Up to that point, the organized movement was quite small, with the main forces coming out of the radicalized student milieu. However, by organizing and publicizing the right kind of broad action, the turnout of more than 50,000 women in cities and towns all over the country, in the first nationwide action ever to be organized by this movement, was a striking example of the widespread support that the women's liberation movement can mobilize.

The August 26 actions helped to cut through the elitist myth that only a handful of middle-class women could understand and act against their oppression as women. Secretaries, high school women, Black women, women from all walks of life turned out on that day.

By putting forward its demands clearly and by demonstrating for them, the feminist movement showed on August 26 that it was fighting for goals which are wanted and needed by masses of women. August 26 demonstrated the impact of the feminist movement and began to show masses of women the serious nature and potential power of the movement.

August 26 was an example of the real meaning of sisterhood—that is, the concept that women can unite together as sisters on the basis of common *struggle*. It provided a feeling of solidarity, of power, and inspired women to see that their problems were shared by masses of others.

It put the onus for the lack of abortion, child care

and equality of job opportunity squarely where it belongs—on the capitalist government.

Women on August 26 were doing exactly what they have been trained not to do. They were out fighting for their own needs, putting these needs first, demanding these needs be met.

August 26 was only one of the first steps in the struggle to build a mass women's liberation movement. This struggle will be a prolonged process with many twists and turns, successes and setbacks. Only through the experience of struggling for feminist demands—by seeing concretely how the power of women can win concessions, and by seeing how the ruling class will try to hedge on and retreat from granting these concessions—will large numbers of women gain the political understanding that is necessary to carry the battle through to a successful conclusion.

Opponents of a mass action perspective

Opponents of the perspective of building a mass-action women's liberation movement around feminist demands include both reformists and ultralefts.

Reformism in the women's movement is based on the belief that it is possible to win liberation under capitalism, and logically leads to dependence on those responsible for perpetuating this system to grant liberation. It leads away from the independent organization of women to fight for the needs of women, and thus away from mass struggle aimed at the capitalist state.

The ultralefts reject struggles around the basic demands of the feminist movement on the grounds that these demands do not explicitly oppose the capitalist system. Because they do not see the revolutionary dynamic of struggles around concrete issues such as child care, abortion, maternity leaves, equal pay, etc., they have no program which can mobilize masses of women who do not yet see their enemy as the capitalist system itself.

Both ultraleftism and reformism make the fundamental error of ignoring the most important task of women's liberation: that is, the creation of a powerful mass, independent women's movement. Neither sees the dynamic relationship between struggles for immediate gains around issues like abortion that directly affect women and the attainment of full female liberation.

The anti–mass action tendencies in the feminist movement can be roughly divided into four different categories. The first category is those ultraleft women who came out of the "new-left" or ex-SDS milieu. The second includes two kinds of utopian idealists: counterinstitutionalists and what can be designated as "livingroom feminists." The third is the traditional-type reformists and liberals. And the fourth category includes several "socialist" tendencies, the largest of these being the Communist Party.

The ultralefts

Many of the founders of the first feminist groups around the country were women who came out of SDS or its general milieu, and they often brought with them the sectarian and ultraleft views of SDS. A good number of these women have remained active in the feminist movement, and while their ideology has gone through considerable flux and change, there are a number of main ideas which characterize their approach.

They hunt for shortcuts around the long, hard job of building a mass movement. To the revolutionary perspective of organizing struggles around the basic needs of women, they *counterpose* "anti-imperialist" or "socialist" sloganeering. They often insist that the feminist movement must, from its very inception, be consciously socialist or anticapitalist. For example, the Chicago Women's Liberation Union has written into its statement of purpose that all members must be anticapitalist.

Another characteristic of these forces is the attempt to turn the women's liberation movement away from fighting for feminist demands by insisting on substituting other issues and demands for them. For example, at one point last fall some groups turned all their energies toward organizing for the Black Panther Party convention in Washington and discontinued activities which would bring new women into the feminist movement. Many of these women also reject student struggles around feminist issues on the false grounds that these struggles are not important to the most oppressed and exploited layers of women.

Utopian idealists

A second major group has been quite aptly designated as "livingroom feminists." The main characteristic of this tendency is that they want to make the movement a substitute for the inability of capitalist society to create an unalienated personal life. They orient toward making women's centers into "living room-like" areas, where small groups can meet together in supposedly unalienated relationships, and they become nervous when more women get together than could fit into a living room. Cell-16 in Boston is one example of this tendency to reject any kind of large-scale organization of women.

Common among livingroom feminists is a hostility to materialist explanations of female oppression. Most of them believe that the oppression of women has grown up in society, not as a result of class oppression, but because men took advantage of the fact that women had the children in order to make slaves of them, and because men personally benefit from the subjugation of women. Many see the oppression of women as being the basis for all the different types of oppression of capitalist society.

Because many livingroom feminists think that female oppression stems from the way individual men and women think, they tend to concentrate on small-group consciousness raising as the chief method for changing society. They believe that liberation can come from changing people's minds, as opposed to changing social institutions.

Relationships between individual men and women in this society are not relationships between equals; and individual men are often the direct agents of perpetrating many forms of discrimination and oppression from which women suffer. The women's movement, however, cannot be aimed at simply trying to change men, or to make them renounce their privileges, any more than the Black liberation movement can succeed if it is aimed at "reforming" whites. All forms of male chauvinism and sexism must be condemned and fought against, and the existence of a powerful feminist movement will have an impact on men and help force them to change. But any orientation of the women's liberation movement towards attempting to create unalienated, completely fulfilling human relationships under capitalism is doomed to failure. It can only end in frustration because it is impossible for either men *or* women to completely remake themselves in this society.

In relation to the question of "renouncing privileges" and attempting to create an unalienated atmosphere within the feminist movement, the livingroom feminists and the new left ultralefts have much in common. Both counterpose the necessity of intellectually understanding one's oppression to a perspective of mass action to end it. Both reacted to August 26 in a sectarian manner. They felt that the women marching there were "low level," and didn't understand their full oppression. They felt that the demands raised on August 26 "weren't radical enough." Both also tended to reject alliances around August 26 with groups such as the National Organization for Women (NOW) because they disagreed with many of the women in NOW on other questions.

Related to the livingroom feminist approach is the perspective of changing society by building counterinstitutions, that is trying to create islands of a perfect new society within the context of the old society. The counterinstitutionists oppose making demands on the government or on existing institutions of society. Instead, they say, women should use their own resources to set up child care centers, abortion counseling, private women's liberation health clinics, clothing exchanges, food co-ops and loan societies. There have been some benefits to a few women from such activities. But the building of counterinstitutions is no alternative to—and is often a conscious retreat from—building a mass women's movement to win liberation.

The women's liberation movement by itself does not have the basic economic resources to meet the needs of masses of women. For example, it is possible through abortion counseling and small-scale abortion clinics to provide for some needs of a limited number of women. But the goal of the feminist movement must be to struggle for the right of *every* woman to have control over her body. And it is only possible to do this by fighting to see that hospitals and medical facilities are used to this end. Similarly, it is necessary to fight for *control* of the educational complexes and facilities, as well as the industries and businesses which discriminate against women.

The attempt to change society through the creation of counterinstitutions reflects a middle class and utopian outlook. It is only the relatively privileged women who have the resources and time to create their own child care centers and other institutions. Moreover, if the counterinstitutions are built with a "serve the people" perspective of providing for working women and poor women and children, this orients the movement in the direction of philanthropic social work.

The heart of the struggle for liberation is not towards counterinstitutionism, but towards fighting to wrest the vast resources of the richest country in the world away from the ruling class, so that these can be used for the greatest welfare of human beings. Anything less than this political struggle means coexistence with an exploitative system which continues to make its basic decisions on the basis of what is profitable to the ruling class.

A parallel error is that of attempting to find personal liberation through the formation of collectives and communes. One of the most powerful aspects of the current radicalization of women has been the rejection of the kinds of dehumanizing relationships imposed on men, women and children by capitalist society. The experimentation with collectives and communes is an example of this rejection and an effort to find something better. But these attempts can have no chance of success as an alternative to the capitalist system because, even in communal living arrangements, some still have to perform alienating labor outside the commune to support nonworking members, and some—often the women—have to prepare food, wash clothes, clean, and take care of children. Until this society is transformed into one in which production is organized on the basis of human needs, and not private profit, it is utopian to think women can win complete liberation.

Liberals

The third basic political category within the movement is composed of the traditional liberals and reformists who rely on the Democratic and Republican parties to change society. Most prominent among these nonsocialist reformists are some women in NOW, and such capitalist politicians as Bella Abzug. We can anticipate that the efforts of the liberals to orient the movement toward support for capitalist party politicians will increase as the feminist movement grows and becomes more of a force. This pressure has a cyclical character, rising as elections approach, receding in years when there are no major political contests. As we approach the 1972 elections we can expect that the "off the streets and into capitalist party politics" pressure will increase.

Instead of supporting capitalist party candidates, the feminist movement must expose these parties which are among the main institutions upholding this sexist, racist, capitalist society. Women have nothing to gain by working through the Democratic or Republican parties, or by supporting "lesser evil" or women candidates within those parties. The Democratic and Republican parties are completely controlled by the capitalist class of this country, and are structured to perpetuate this control. Any attempt to work within these parties will contribute to the illusions that masses of women have about the system. The job of revolutionary women is not to reinforce the illusions that masses of people have in the capitalist ruling parties, but to expose the fact that these parties and the economic system they represent cannot provide liberation.

Many of the women in the feminist movement who orient at one time or another to the Democratic Party, either through lobbying or campaigning for a political candidate, are women who can be involved in building independent mass actions around basic women's liberation demands. Although these women will often switch back and forth—depending in part on whether it's an election year or not—they can often be won to support mass actions. Some of these women can become convinced through their experiences that the Democratic Party is a trap, and we can expect to win many of them to a revolutionary perspective.

Communist Party, Progressive Labor, International Socialists

Without exception, all the reformist "socialist" tendencies have exhibited one or another degree of hostility towards the women's liberation movement.

Progressive Labor completely rejects the feminist movement on the basis that the only valid women's struggles are those which are waged by women workers around narrowly conceived job issues.

International Socialists have a more confused approach, which changes from time to time and is different in different parts of the country. But all of their various wings fail to understand the full revolutionary implications of the rise of the new feminism. They underestimate the role which students and young women out of the student milieu can play in initiating and building the movement, and they try to orient to what they narrowly conceive of as struggles which relate to working women.

The Communist Party in a whole series of articles and statements has shown quite openly its hostility toward feminism. Their attitude is expressed most clearly in their assertions that the feminist struggle is less important than other movements and in their reactionary defense of, and romanticization of, the family.

The Communist Party's hostile attitude toward feminism flows from their general perspective of supporting the Soviet bureaucracy's attempts to co-exist peacefully with world capitalism, their reformist perspective for all American mass movements and their defense of the Soviet bureaucracy's reactionary domestic policies. For one thing, feminism represents a challenge to the subordinate place of women in the Soviet Union. It doesn't take a feminist very long to figure out that the role played by women in Soviet society is not what we are fighting for.

Secondly, the CP fears all potential mass struggles in this country which could pose a real threat to the ruling class and upset the world equilibrium of the "great powers." The Communist Party does not see this period as a time when forces capable of actually making a revolution are being assembled and organized independent of the ruling class. As they see it, the perspective we have before us in this country is not one of revolution, but of assuring the ascendency of the liberal, pro–peaceful coexistence wing of the capitalist class. They think of all independent movements against oppression in terms of how they can channel them into acting in support of, and as a pressure on, the liberal wing of the capitalist class. They are afraid of feminism because—like the nationalism of the oppressed nationalities—it poses itself so sharply against not only the conservatives, but the liberals as well.

What the CP fears most is a mass, fighting women's movement which struggles for "unreasonable" demands which the capitalist liberals cannot meet. And they are the strongest opponents of the perspective of building such a movement. We know that as the movement grows bigger they will adapt to it more and more and their opposition will become more astute. They will use both sectarian and ultraleft and utopian approaches as well as try to orient the movement toward giving support to Democratic Party candidates such as Shirley Chisholm and Bella Abzug.

All four of the above political categories are united in one way: they are all opposed to building the feminist movement in a way which could attract masses of women and orient them toward independent struggle.

The new left, the livingroom feminists and the counterinstitutionists all either organize in such a way as to keep the movement invisible to the masses of women, or around issues which do not relate to their concrete needs.

The reformists, instead of building a mass, independent movement, look ultimately to a reformed or realigned Democratic Party and the capitalist rulers to give women liberation.

Supporters of all four anti–mass action tendencies have, in many cases, used red-baiting attacks against the SWP to cloud over the real political disagreements they have with the SWP and other supporters of a mass action perspective. Instead of taking up the political differences involved, they picture SWPers as socialist dupes of the "male-dominated" left, coming in to "infiltrate" and "take over" the feminist movement.

Such charges are echoes, within the feminist movement, of the charges of the reactionaries during the McCarthy era. The purpose of the red-baiting is to try to *avoid* discussion of the real political issues, to prejudice people against carrying on an open discussion with supporters of a mass-action perspective, by the socialists or not, by branding them as "Reds" or "Trots."

The only way to end such red-baiting is to explain what is really behind it. The issue is not one of the SWP "taking over" the movement in an undemocratic manner, but of real political disagreements. In fact, the SWP has a record of being the most consistent fighter for the maintenance of democratic procedures within the movement.

Red-baiting, and the exclusionism that flows from it, represents a danger to the entire feminist movement by making free, democratic discussion and organization impossible. In carrying out the activities of the feminist movement, it is of great importance that there be clear, calm, democratic discussion of perspectives, unclouded by red-baiting, so that the greatest number of women possible can be informed about the real issues, and can help participate in determining the strategy of the movement, not on the basis of prejudice or hearsay, but on the basis of complete and open discussion.

Our tasks

The feminist movement has experienced an explosive growth in the last two years. From a few small circles meeting together to discuss the deepgoing problems women face in capitalist society, it has already expanded to a movement composed of hundreds of organizations and capable of mobilizing tens of thousands of women in the streets. In addition to all the groups organized around the needs and interests of specific groups of women—high school, campus, gay, Black, Chicana—broad action coalitions have been built in at least a dozen cities and states.

Women in the Socialist Workers Party have participated in the activities of these organizations and done our best to build them and win them to a perspective of organizing and appealing to the broad masses of women.

Around the country the SWP has participated in actions built around all the central demands of the movement. We've been fighting for women's studies, against sexism in advertising, for high school women's rights. We've helped organize Black, Chicana and other Third World women's activities and groups and we have organized to support struggles opposing discrimination against women on the job. Child care is another issue we have helped to organize around, especially in fighting for child care centers on campuses.

In the course of these struggles and experiences, it has become clear that at this time the abortion fight is the issue which is attracting the largest numbers of women and the greatest enthusiasm. Abortion projects and coalitions have sprung up all over the country and many of these groups are reaching out to very broad layers of women, including church groups, unions, and Black groups.

In response to these struggles, opposition to the right of women to have unrestricted access to abortions is also building up. The efforts of many reactionary groups are centered around the anti-abortion fight. The hierarchy of the Catholic Church in particular is investing huge sums of money in this effort, taking out advertisements in newspapers and organizing demonstrations. In those states where liberalized laws have been passed, the legislatures, city governments and conservative forces have continually fought to take back even the limited gains made.

If women are going to continue to win victories in the struggle to gain control over their own bodies, much less prevent the ruling class from taking away those gains already made, the women's liberation movement must make the abortion fight the central focus of activity in the coming period. The feminist movement must intervene decisively in this growing national ferment and discussion over the issue of abortion and focus its energies on mobilizing hundreds of thousands of women to fight for repeal of all laws restricting the right of abortion along with the demand for no forced sterilization. The broadest possible coalitions should be built to carry out the struggle, so that the real feelings and power of the masses of women can be brought to bear. Within this broad mobilization, there is a necessity to educate on the importance of winning *free* abortion on demand, a demand which is in the interest of the great majority of women, and which is necessary if women are to win the complete right to control their own bodies.

Abortion is an issue that affects millions of women in the most immediate way. Victories around this issue will be very important in showing the growing power of the women's liberation movement, in proving to masses of women that the feminist movement is serious, fighting around issues which are of concern to all women. A successful fight to make abortions available to all women would have a tremendously liberating effect and help to raise the whole movement to a higher level. It could serve as an inspiration and an example for struggles over other issues and enable the movement to take the next, powerful step forward around further demands.

Our central task in the period ahead will be

working with other women to inspire and educate about the central political importance of the abortion fight, and building a nationwide abortion movement which can have a real impact and win significant victories for women.

In addition to the fight around the abortion issue there are a number of other specific tasks which are of importance in the coming months.

One is to continue our activity to build the feminist organizations and activities of Black women, Chicanas, Puerto Rican women, and other oppressed nationalities. As the debate on feminism continues to deepen within the nationalist movements we want to continue to be the champions of the position that nationalism and feminism are complementary, not contradictory struggles, that they will strengthen and advance each other. Through our publications, forums, election campaigns, speaking tours and other activities we want to take an active part in this debate.

We also want to continue and deepen our work in building campus-based women's liberation groups, high school organizations, and citywide organizations. Building campus women's liberation groups is a key task, since the campus groups are the largest and fastest growing sector of the movement.

We should continue to educate within the movement on the importance of the war as an issue of vital concern to women. The successes we had in building the April 24 United Women's Contingent are a clear indication of the correctness of this perspective. Those women who are convinced of the need to mobilize and act against the war are going to be among the best builders of a mass feminist movement around other concrete demands of concern to women.

Building the 1971 and 1972 socialist election campaigns is the party's central propaganda vehicle to explain and mobilize around these perspectives. Our party is the only one which fights unequivocally for the liberation of women, and which has a program to achieve that end. Our election campaigns have proved an effective way of reaching out to literally millions of women with the ideas and demands of the feminist movement. Our candidates, both men and women, have become known as campaigners for women's liberation, and our campaigns have played an important role in winning new women to ideas of the SWP. Through women's support committees for the 1972 campaign in particular we will be able to win many women to the revolutionary socialist movement.

In the past months we have put out a tremendous amount of literature about women's liberation, including regular articles in the *Militant* and the *International Socialist Review*. Many of these have been reproduced in pamphlet or book form. The sales of all our literature concerning women's liberation is an important task.

Subscriptions to and sales of individual copies of the *Militant* are especially important because this is the place where we put forward a week-by-week analysis of the perspectives for the movement, where we can help build national campaigns, answer attacks against us or the feminist movement, take part in discussions and raise general consciousness about the roots and causes of women's oppression. And it brings readers our analyses of all the basic political issues of today, giving them a perspective on the relationship between the struggle for women's liberation and the struggle for socialism.

There is an entire range of educational activities we engage in which are of particular importance. In addition to forums and branch educationals on specific questions as they arise, members should be encouraged to read the women's liberation press and consciousness-raising literature. Both external and internal classes on women's liberation should be organized regularly.

Finally, significant numbers of activists in the women's liberation movement have begun to join the SWP and YSA. We have an especially important job in educating these new forces, giving them a thorough grounding in our program and integrating them into all aspects of party activity. The best of the new generation of feminists will be attracted to the Trotskyist movement; our job is to educate them as revolutionary socialist politicians in the fullest sense.

The revolutionary party

The combined power of all the different social struggles which are emerging in this country will be needed to constitute a force strong enough to overthrow American capitalism and establish a workers state, based on and fighting for the needs of the vast majority of the people.

Although the women's liberation movement has the potential of organizing tens of millions of women in independent struggle, it is not by itself capable of destroying the capitalist system and thereby laying the material foundations for the destruction of class society and the liberation of women. Such a successful struggle can only be achieved through the politicalization, radicalization and mobilization of the masses of working people of this country.

Only a revolutionary Marxist party, composed of the most conscious representatives of all the oppressed and exploited sectors of our society, and based on a transitional program capable of mobilizing a mass anticapitalist struggle, can hope to lead this revolutionary struggle to victory. Only such a party can develop a perspective and program for bringing together the diverse struggles that are emerging so that their potential anticapitalist striking power can be unified.

So long as capitalism exists it is impossible for either women or men to gain full dignity and humanity, other than by fighting against oppression. It is with that perspective that we try to win the best of the new generation of feminists to the Socialist Workers Party, to raise their consciousness to revolutionary socialist consciousness, and to organize and inspire the masses of women to fight to change society.

While a socialist revolution is a precondition for the complete liberation of women, a socialist revolution cannot be complete until women are totally free. The development of a powerful women's liberation movement now, before the socialist revolution, means that this movement will not only strengthen the struggle against capitalism, but will also be a powerful stimulus in the period of the construction of the new society to revolutionary changes in the family system and other institutions which oppress women.

The essence of being "feminine" has always meant the opposite of asserting control over one's life. Women have been trained to be passive, weak, submissive, self-sacrificing, gentle, emotional—in short to think of themselves as being powerless as individuals and as a sex. In carrying out the struggle for liberation, women are doing something they have been systematically educated to believe themselves incapable of: women are becoming fighters, leaders, organizers, and clear political thinkers, capable of mobilizing the power of the masses of women in the decisive struggles against the capitalist system.

EMERGENCE OF A NEW FEMINIST MOVEMENT
Excerpt from 'Perspectives and Lessons of the New Radicalization'
Political resolution adopted by the SWP national convention, August 1971

Growth of the feminist movement
The year 1970 saw the beginning of the transformation of the new feminist movement into a mass movement with appeal to the broadest layers of American women. It has already had a deep impact on the political consciousness of the country, as reflected in the mass media and in the spread of the women's liberation movement to every nook and cranny of the nation. Women in all kinds of situations—in Black and Chicano organizations, unions, educational institutions, churches, professional organizations, in workplaces—have raised and struggled for feminist demands. The potential power of this movement exists in virtually every organization and institution of American society.

The August 26 marches, commemorating the right-to-vote victory achieved by the first mass mobilization of feminism in the U.S., were the first nationwide mass actions of the new women's liberation movement. The publicity around these actions popularized the movement and its demands to millions of Americans. They demonstrated the power and potential of mobilizing women around democratic and transitional demands that both attack the pressing manifestations of the oppression millions of women suffer and that lead in the direction of the complete liberation of women.

The mass-mobilization approach, confirmed in action on August 26, points the way forward for the movement. It is the revolutionary alternative to any tendencies to turn inward and stagnate in a small-circle existence; or to reject feminist demands under the guise of adopting an "anti-imperialist" or "workers" orientation, which has been evident in ultraleft currents of the women's movement; or to depend on the liberals, as proposed by the reformists.

The three basic demands of the women's liberation movement form a starting point for the development of a transitional program for women's liberation.

The first of these, free abortion on demand, coupled with opposition to forced sterilization, is based upon the elementary and democratic right of women to control their own bodies. This right is of immediate concern to most women, and is a life-and-death question for hundreds of thousands of women every year. The thrust of this demand cuts sharply into basic and deep-going cultural, social, and religious prejudices against women; it is aimed at the subordinate and dependent role women have been subjected to since the rise of class society. The part of this demand that calls for *free* abortion on demand goes beyond democratic demands: it raises the concept of socialization of medical care and answers a need of the most oppressed and exploited.

Reactionary forces, mobilizing against the women's movement in opposition to this demand, are attempting to reverse the partial victories the movement has already scored concerning abortion. The political struggles around abortion will be one of the important battles of the entire next stage of the women's liberation movement.

The second major demand of the movement, for free, community-controlled, twenty-four-hour child-care centers available to all, answers a pressing need of millions of women, especially working women. At the same time, it highlights the importance of society's responsibility for rearing the young.

The third demand centers on pay, educational and job opportunities, and legal rights for women equal to those of men. These democratic demands challenge capitalism's economic and political institutionalization of the subordinate and dependent status of women, which has its roots in the historical rise of the patriarchal family system. They put forward a concept indispensable for inspiring and mobilizing a powerful movement for women's liberation: that is, the full and complete worth and dignity of women.

The women's liberation movement has already had a profound impact on the current radicalization, not only by adding another sector of militants to the struggle, but also through the implications of its critical analysis of the historical role of the institution of the nuclear family. This institution, which has its origins in the rise of class society and which, in one form or another, has been a necessary feature of all class societies, plays the central role in implanting in infants and children the ideology and character structure necessary to maintain the hierarchical, exploitative, and alienated social relations intrinsic to capitalism.

The women's liberation movement thus brings to light and helps break down some of the deepest prejudices and attitudes among the ideological and moral props of class rule. It raises problems of human alienation, whose solution lies in the establishment of a workers' state and the building of socialism. It intensifies the struggle to expose the moral bankruptcy of the ruling class and to heighten the moral authority of the fighting mass movements.

By participating in this movement, women are transforming their view of themselves, affirming the essential dignity and worth denied them through the entire period of class society. An integral part of the fight against capitalism is the fight against the racism and sexism built into the ideology of capitalism. This discovery and rethinking by women of their history and worth has paralleled the same phenomenon among the oppressed nationalities. It has reawakened a demand for knowledge and understanding of their oppression—its history, causes, and the road to its elimination. It previews a similar process that will take place in the workers' radicalization.

The responsiveness of the Socialist Workers Party and Young Socialist Alliance to the rise of the new feminism has been another important test of our movement. Our ability to embrace this movement as our own, to participate in it and learn from it, and to help lead it in the direction of the mass independent mobilization of women around democratic and transitional demands stands in sharp contrast to the default of all our opponents who claim to be socialist or communist.

STRUGGLES BY WOMEN REFLECT THE DEPTH OF THE SOCIAL CRISIS AND RADICALIZATION

Excerpts from political resolution adopted by the SWP national convention, August 1975

FROM PART IV: 'CHANGING CHARACTER AND COMPOSITION OF THE WORKING CLASS'

Women

The increase in the percentage of women in the work force has been one of the biggest changes brought about by American capital in the postwar period.

In 1930 women constituted only 20 percent of the work force, and less than 25 percent of all women of working age were employed. By 1945, largely because of the needs of the war industry, women constituted 30 percent of the work force, and more than a third of all women of working age were employed. But by 1972 women constituted 37 percent of the work force, and 44 percent of all women were employed.

While the decade following World War II saw a small decline in the number of women in industry and employment, reversing some of the gains established during the war years, by 1955 the curve of employment began to climb again. The last twenty years have seen a steady rise in female employment. During the boom of the 1960s two-thirds of all new jobs created were taken by women. This rate of increase in female employment occurred because of the rapid rate of expansion of the economy as a whole.

The highest percentage of working women, while classified by the government as "white collar," went into the fastest growing sectors of the working class—office workers, service employees, sales, public workers, and teachers.

Toward the end of the postwar boom, through the enforcement of quotas and affirmative action suits, women even began to win a slightly larger percentage of jobs in basic industry.

Forty percent of all working women are either the sole or major wage earners in their households. At the same time, working wives are the single largest source of the "affluence" of many American working-class families.

The growing integration of women into the work force has brought with it a heightening of class consciousness among women. As they increasingly see themselves as long-term and permanent members of the work force and are recognized as such by others, the need to protect their jobs and working conditions by joining unions and bringing their militancy to bear in the labor movement becomes more obvious and urgent. This is part of the process that has given rise to formations such as women's committees in the unions and the Coalition of Labor Union Women.

FROM PART V: 'RADICALIZATION AND MOBILIZATION OF THE ALLIES OF THE PROLETARIAT'

Women

Women constitute both a growing percentage of the working class and an increasingly important ally of the working class. Women are not a minority. They constitute more than one-half the population and are not restricted to any geographical area, social stratum, or occupation. Like the American population as a whole, they are increasingly proletarian in composition.

Sexism is also one of the main ideological tools by which the ruling class keeps the working class divided, weakening class consciousness and unity, and reinforcing reactionary religious and obscurantist ideology.

Widespread acceptance of the idea that "woman's place is in the home" is used to promote the myth that women do not seek employment out of necessity but out of choice. The consignment of women to the home keeps a reservoir of extra labor available and reduces the social costs and consequences of large numbers of periodically unemployed women.

The oppression of all women as a sex, like national oppression, creates a pariah section of the industrial reserve army, a labor pool whose super-exploitation generates high rates of surplus value, helps drive down the wage level of all workers, and weakens the labor movement.

The oppression of women as a sex does not stem from the particular needs of capitalism alone. Its historic origins go back to the dawn of class society. Sexism is the necessary ideological underpinning of the maintenance of the family as an institution of class rule. The family is a primary mechanism for inculcating authoritarian, hierarchical attitudes into each new generation. It is the institution to which the rulers abdicate social responsibility and care for the young, the old, the sick, and the unemployed, and to which they shift the burden of economic crisis and breakdown—a burden felt especially keenly by the working class.

The struggle for women's liberation poses the problem of the total reorganization of society from its smallest repressive unit (the family) to its largest (the state). The liberation of women demands a thoroughgoing reorganization of society's productive and reproductive institutions in order to maximize social welfare and bring about a truly human existence for all.

The search for solutions to the issues raised by women's liberation is one of the driving forces of the coming American revolution. The ability of the workers' vanguard to provide clear and concrete answers to the questions posed by capitalism's oppression of women and to fight for their realization will be decisive in mobilizing the forces necessary to overturn capitalism.

Women's liberation movement

A women's liberation movement emerged in the late 1960s with a political character and social depth vastly different from the forms through which women participated in the last working-class radicalization, in the 1930s. Three processes—developing over the postwar decades—led to this resurgence.

• The large-scale integration of women into the labor force and the significant rise in the general educational level that accompanied this process.

• The growing realization among millions of people that the development of the productive and technical capacities of industry and science has now made possible unlimited abundance and the socialization of "women's work" if society is rationally organized and planned.

• The challenge to bourgeois social and moral norms, a consequence of the broad radicalization, made it possible for significant numbers of women to develop as organizers and political leaders.

All of these conditions converged at the end of the 1960s when the antiwar movement and student radicalization were at their height. Many of the initial organizers of the women's groups came out of these movements. The rapid spread of the movement, its deep reverberations through all layers of society, penetrating into the organized labor movement, attested to the ripeness of the conditions that bred it.

Because of women's distribution throughout society, and the radical character of the questions posed, the rise of the women's liberation movement has already deeply affected mass consciousness and every aspect of culture in the broadest sense of the term. Literature, TV, movies, and other avenues have felt its impact. There is a tendency to challenge all values and mores and to review all aspects of existence, every facet of society by looking at them through women's eyes.

The most basic assumptions of class society about women are being carefully scrutinized and rejected by millions of women and men. The ferment over the woman question today recalls the radicalization of the Debsian pre–World War I period, or even the pre–Civil War radicalization, where the specific question of women's role in society was also a distinct component of the general social ferment—although on a much more restricted practical and theoretical basis. The vanguard role of women in other social movements is also parallel.

Struggles by women directed toward their emancipation are among the clearest indicators of the depth of the current *social* crisis and radicalization. The fact that these struggles began to emerge *before* the effects of a major economic crisis were felt confirms this all the more emphatically.

Progress and reaction

The large increase in the percentage of employed women, in the number of women who are heads of households, and in the unionization of working women, combined with the rise of the women's liberation movement, has created a difficult problem for the ruling class. The acceptability of the use of women as reserve labor—the vast majority of women who drop out of the labor market in hard times are not even counted as unemployed—has been diminished.

As with the oppressed nationalities, the road toward true equality and equal opportunity for women lies through preferential treatment—quotas and affirmative action in industry, education, politics, and society—to correct the inequality of opportunity established by centuries of discrimination.

Thus, the attempt by the ruling class to wipe out the gains that oppressed national minorities and women made through preferential hiring and upgrading victories is an important part of the political and economic counteroffensive mounted by the Democrats and Republicans. And the resistance of women to being shoved out of work on the basis of last hired, first fired is growing. There has been rising opposition among women to having seniority rights broken by maternity leave, being denied access to apprenticeship programs for skilled or "heavy" jobs, receiving unequal pay, or being denied the right to participate in bargaining units because of "part-time" classifications.

The radicalization of women and the examples of direct action by others in the last decade have made housewives react with anger and frustration to the economic squeeze on their budgets and have led them to be more inclined to try to do something about it themselves. The 1973 meat boycott and the popularity of consumer investigations like those of Ralph Nader are harbingers of the protests to come.

The challenge to the bourgeois social order represented by the rise of the women's liberation movement means that the gains won by women have become a major target of reaction, second only to the Black movement. In Boston the anti-busing drive, the attempt to reverse the right to abortion, and the anti-ERA demonstrations have provided an instructive example of the combination of targets selected in the country as a whole by the most rabid reactionary forces.

The right to abortion and constitutional and legislative guarantees of equal rights for women, as obvious as they may seem to some, represent a challenge to class society and its entire ideological superstructure. The protectors of the bourgeois order know this. They will continue to try to chip away at all such gains.

Many of the initial participants in the women's liberation movement rapidly faced a crisis of perspectives. Some were won to revolutionary Marxism. Others went in the direction of ultraleftism or forms of personal escapism. Still more were drawn into the two-party game of capitalist politics, where the ruling class was again quick to create openings for leaders of the movement.

Like the withdrawal of troops from Vietnam and abolition of the draft, the Supreme Court decision to legalize early abortions was part of the ruling class's general attempt to defuse the radicalization and eliminate some of the issues that had become focal points for mass mobilizations.

But the abortion victory, as with other democratic concessions to women, can not eliminate the roots of the oppression of women or defuse their struggle for long. On the contrary, while such gains may lead to temporary lulls or downturns in mass action, over time they only serve to generate new demands and to create more favorable conditions for building an independent mass feminist movement capable of mobilizing women in struggle against their oppression.

THE FIGHT FOR AN INDEPENDENT WOMEN'S MOVEMENT
Report adopted by the SWP National Committee, February 25, 1978

by Willie Mae Reid

The theme of this plenum—the turn in the turn—as spelled out in preceding reports, will mean a powerful strengthening of our participation in the women's liberation movement. It means stepping up our ability to bring our program for women's liberation into the organizations of the working class. It means increasing our ability to involve working-class women, particularly those of the oppressed nationalities, in women's liberation activities.

More and more we will be speaking within the women's movement as industrial workers and unionists. And, likewise, on the job and in the unions as feminists. The result can only enhance our ability to explain and convince women of our perspectives for the women's movement and increase our ability to reach them wherever they are, including ERA coalitions, campus groups, reproductive freedom coalitions, anti-*Bakke* groups, the Coalition of Labor Union Women (CLUW), or the National Organization for Women (NOW).

The framework in which to discuss the current situation in the women's movement is the continuing and deepening political derailment of the movement, expressed in the class-collaborationist policies of the leadership of NOW. It is the largest, most authoritative women's organization in the country and, for that reason, the organization whose misleadership poses the major obstacle to mobilizing women in defense of their rights. This is what made it necessary to begin a debate in NOW for a correct political course for the women's movement.

This discussion began prior to the national NOW conference in April 1977. But it could not have clarified the issues in just a few months. Nor was its purpose to quickly secure a majority in NOW around one or another issue. A far-ranging discussion on perspectives for the women's movement was needed, and time was required to hold it.

This report will concentrate on NOW, assessing where the organization stands and what we can anticipate between now and next October, when NOW will hold its next national conference.

But focusing the report on NOW doesn't mean that women's liberation work in unions, such as the Steelworkers, District 31; in women's committees; in CLUW; on the job; and on the campuses is not important. Our perspective in CLUW, for example, is to continue to encourage women unionists to join and build it and to look for opportunities to involve more and more trade-union women in women's rights activities.

Working class in action

As far as the women's liberation movement is concerned, the most important thing happening in the country today is the coal miners' strike. The miners' resistance to the operators' offensive and the outcome of that battle will have an impact on winning the ERA, reclaiming abortion rights for all women, securing affirmative-action programs and other women's rights—all of the issues that NOW must address.

The political perspective we support in the women's movement is based on our understanding that the struggle for women's liberation is part of the class struggle and must be carried out on a class-struggle program. The movement must mobilize women and their allies to defend women's rights. This requires a leadership that refuses to subordinate the interests of women to the demands of ruling-class politicians.

We're trying to explain and to convince women's rights fighters that it is precisely the absence of this kind of consistent feminist perspective in the women's movement that has allowed the government to deal blows against past gains. The leadership crisis in the women's movement is part of a more general crisis of leadership in the workers movement that has made it possible for the capitalists and their two parties to carry out the offensive against the rights and living standards of the working class.

The general relationship of class forces determines what we can and what we can't accomplish in the battle for our rights. The miners' determined fight gives a powerful example of resistance that will inspire Blacks, other oppressed nationalities, women, other unionists and industrial workers, on a much broader scale than Steelworkers Fight Back did in the unions. Carter's intervention in the strike negotiations when the coal operators' second proposed contract was overwhelmingly rejected by the miners exposes the cold-blooded calculations of the ruling class and the steps their government will take when workers refuse to bow to the rules of class-collaborationist strategy.

There are few in the women's movement today—certainly few in NOW—who understand what stake women have in the outcome of the miners' strike. But as the issues are posed more clearly every day, that will make it possible to find ways to link women's struggle for equality to the miners' demands for better working conditions and protection of their hard-won benefits such as their health cards.

Women support 'Bakke' actions

Changes in the scope of the forces expected to be involved in the April 15 national action to overturn the *Bakke* decision do not change the importance of the political campaign we are engaged in to educate and mobilize the women's movement in the fight to defend affirmative action and to reverse the *Bakke* decision.

Involving women in the anti-*Bakke* actions is one of the most important things we've been doing in this work. It's a political challenge to help counter the deep confusion in the women's movement and elsewhere over the need to support special steps to make up for past—and present—race and sex discrimination against women and the oppressed national minorities.

The call by the National Committee to Overturn the Bakke Decision (NCOBD) for spring actions to reverse the *Bakke* ruling provides an opportunity to convince the women's movement that the *Bakke* ruling is an assault on *every* woman's right to equal educational and employment opportunities, just as the Hyde amendment, directed against women on Medicaid, is an attack on the abortion rights of *all* women. The local actions being organized to protest *Bakke* provide a focus for bringing the women's movement into joint action with its allies among Blacks and other oppressed nationalities and in the labor movement.

Steps to participate in these actions have already been taken by NOW chapters and women's groups in cities and on campuses across the country. NOW chapter program nights, speak-outs, panel discussions, conferences, and workshops on the meaning of *Bakke* for women have already been organized during the week of February 19–25 and on March 8, International Women's Day.

At the same time, other local activities may lend themselves to building anti-*Bakke* support, like the actions usually called in early April in the Black community to commemorate the assassination of Martin Luther King, Jr.

Women comrades in unions can also win anti-*Bakke* support in the labor movement. Discussions with coworkers on the job and in trade-union women's and civil rights committees; educational panels at union meetings; resolutions in opposition to *Bakke*—like the one passed in District 31 of the United Steelworkers of America—are all ways of involving labor in actions with the women's movement and the Black movement to protest *Bakke*.

The key is to take advantage of the opportunity to organize the women's liberation movement to participate in the activities called in support of affirmative action leading up to and including April 15.

Capitalist offensive

The capitalist offensive against women's rights, in general, has broadened and increased during the last year.

In addition to attacks on affirmative action, the Hyde amendment, cutting off government funds for abortion, went into effect this summer. Over the fall, Congress debated the differences in the ruling class on how much to restrict abortion rights. This long, drawn-out debate culminated in reaffirming the Hyde amendment. But, the debate was aimed at wearing down the women's movement, eroding support for legal abortion, and trying to make women grateful that the blow to their rights was not more severe.

The passage of the Hyde amendment has had an impact on young women, women of the oppressed nationalities, and other low-income women. This has been hidden by the capitalist media. But the few reports that have come out tell how frightened and humiliated women become trying to raise funds for legal abortions, and how this delays the procedure, which becomes more difficult after the first three months of pregnancy. The reports tell how more women are being forced to bring pregnancies to term. And they tell of women who have died from illegal abortions.

The offensive against women's rights has also prevented any new states from ratifying the Equal Rights Amendment. With the deadline for passage set for March 22, 1979, and three more states still needed to ratify, organizing the majority support that exists for the ERA becomes an increasingly urgent task, which I will return to later in this report.

Carter's State of the Union address this past January was a signal that the everyday lives of working people will get worse and that their hopes for improvement in these conditions are not part of the ruling class's projections. It was a forewarning of fresh attacks that will affect women, further pushing back gains previously won, with the intention of establishing a more reactionary "public consensus" on the limits of women's equality.

Response to attacks

How have women responded to these attacks?

Although unorganized and hamstrung by the current misleadership of the women's movement, the reaction by women indicates that consciousness of the ruling-class offensive and resistance to it is deepening.

The clearest expression of this resistance was the Houston International Women's Year conference (IWY) in November. Although tightly controlled by the Carter administration, delegates at the conference overwhelmingly adopted stands objectively counterposed to the ruling-class attacks: support to government funding of abortion, to the ERA, to civil rights for gays and lesbians, and to other measures to ensure equality for women. A significant aspect of the conference was the clear profeminist stand taken by women of the oppressed nationalities.

The conference helped legitimize the women's movement before the millions who watched it on TV or read the extensive newspaper accounts of it. This media event was an inspiration particularly for women and a reflection of the continuing radicalization among them.

Another sign of the strong desire of women to defend their rights was the wave of protests over the summer and fall against the Hyde amendment. Although modest in size, these were widespread, often organized through broad coalitions that included some local NOW chapters. These actions represented a step forward in recognizing the threat to all women's abortion rights and in taking action against the attacks.

Similarly, the turnout of more than 3,000 pro-ERA supporters—many of them trade unionists—for the Richmond, Virginia, demonstration in January showed the growing willingness of women workers to help lead the struggle for women's rights.

A significant layer of younger Black women, Chicanas, Puertorriqueñas, and Asian-American women participated in the fall anti-*Bakke* actions. This ferment among women of the oppressed nationalities continues to be expressed in the sharp debate in the Black community provoked by the play by Black poet Ntozake Shange, "For Colored Girls Who Have Considered Suicide When the Rainbow Is Enuf." The play, on a tour of several cities, is a powerful statement against the oppression of Black women.

Chicana feminists continue to come together to discuss their oppression as women. A Chicana conference has already been scheduled this spring in California.

Lesbian feminists are also increasing their efforts to address the oppression they face as women. They played prominent roles in the massive protests last June following the defeat for gay rights in Miami, Florida. The lesbian caucuses were among the most militant and best organized at the state and national IWY conferences. They succeeded in adding opposition to discrimination on the basis of sexual preference to the "national plan of action," as well as in generating discussion in Houston on the importance to the women's movement of support for gay rights.

An important sign of the ferment among women is the influx of new members into NOW. *National Now Times* reports 20,000 new members between the April NOW conference and the IWY conference in November. This reflects the desire of more and more women to openly identify with feminism by joining a women's rights organization.

NOW leaders move right

How has the new leadership of NOW evolved in the crisis?

A series of articles by Mary-Alice Waters and Cindy Jaquith in the *Militant* last summer characterized the April conference as a turning point for NOW. Those articles explained that the new leadership elected there and the political resolutions it succeeded in passing represented a perspective of deepening NOW's dependence on the Democratic Party as the supposed road to women's equality. The authors pointed to the political action committees and the ERA Strike Force in NOW as the major vehicles established to carry out this course. They explained that this was a serious step away from building an independent women's movement. It is a step, instead, toward imposing a more explicit class-collaborationist approach. Concessions for women are sought through "moderation": by playing according to the rules made by the capitalist politicians; by refusing to challenge the status quo; and by proving their loyalty to the capitalist two-party system. The course adopted was one that would further demobilize the women's movement and compromise on the fundamental demands of the women's rights struggle.

From its standpoint, in order to turn NOW into an organization with "clout" inside the two-party system, the new leadership had to change the organization's image from a "radical" feminist group to one that is more "responsible." Consolidating NOW into such an organization means a drive to force political homogeneity around a much more open pro-capitalist party perspective and to strengthen the organization's apparatus.

But we also noted that there was real opposition to such a course in NOW, which was reflected, for example, in the close vote on the Political Action Committees resolution (PACs) at the April conference. And, we said, in order to impose this perspective on the entire membership, NOW leaders would have to change the character of NOW by curtailing the democratic rights of its members and the traditional way local NOW chapters have decided their own priorities.

Our assessment of the meaning of the April conference has turned out to be dead right. Since then, the leadership has taken substantial steps toward their goals. Their progress is evident in the organizational changes they have made in NOW's functioning.

The national office was moved from New York City to Washington, D.C., and has a full-time paid staff, which makes regular trips to area NOW meetings. Salaried field organizers coordinate the activities of the ERA Strike Force and function as the link between the national office and the local chapters.

The national newspaper, renamed the *National NOW Times*, has become a professional publication with articles written to organize chapter activities around the leadership's political perspective. A national Minority Women's Steering Committee and a public relations apparatus to enhance NOW's visibility in the media have been set up.

Many of these changes could be helpful in strengthening NOW's ability to mobilize its membership into action in defense of women's rights. However, they have been used by the national leadership for a different purpose: to coalesce the organization around the strategy of dependence on the capitalist politicians by projecting lobbying, letter writing, and campaigning to elect "good" politicians and defeat "bad" ones—what the leaders call "negative campaigning" and the "vengeance" strategy.

These organizational changes have been used to try to eliminate the local autonomy traditional in NOW and to impose the line of the national leadership on local chapters. This can be seen most clearly in the recent ERA articles carried by the *National NOW Times*.

NOW leaders have laid out a three-pronged approach: (1) a lobbying campaign to urge Congress to extend the 1979 deadline for the ERA; (2) a boycott campaign that involves getting large organizations not to hold conventions in unratified states; and (3) campaigning for pro-ERA capitalist candidates in the 1978 legislative elections.

ERA extension campaign

With March 1979 fast approaching, it is clear that extension of the ratification deadline for the ERA would give the women's movement more time to actually build a movement that could force ERA ratification. We support the deadline extension. The question, however, is *how* to fight for extension and on what axis.

NOW leaders approach the question within the framework of their orientation to the two capitalist parties. And consequently they draw the wrong conclusions about why the ERA has not been ratified. They see the "problem" as a few men in the state legislatures—and not their own refusal to mobilize women in action. In fact, they propose deepening this strategy of dependence on the capitalist politicians in order to win an extension.

The deadline extension campaign they have outlined boils down to a high-powered lobbying effort where more members will spend hours each week writing hundreds of postcards to Jimmy Carter and their congressional representatives and planning vacations in Washington, D.C., so they can lobby there. Currently, time is set aside at NOW chapter meetings to fill out preprinted postcards.

Writing in *Majority Report,* an independent feminist newspaper published in New York City, NOW President Eleanor Smeal explained recently that one of the aims of this campaign is to pinpoint who among the Democrats and Republicans will vote for the extension, with the implied threat that those who don't will be turned out of office in the fall elections if their terms are up.

Absent from the extension "strategy" is any perspective for bringing ERA supporters into the streets in an ongoing action campaign. That's the only proposal that can win extension or ratification of the ERA, the only one that can even attract enthusiastic support in the membership. In fact, the level of frustration from filling out postcards has already begun to rise among NOW members.

ERA boycott

The second prong of the leadership's ERA strategy consists of encouraging a tourist boycott of the unratified states.

The boycott has had some minimal effect, but as long as it is projected as a substitute for a mass-action approach, instead of a complement to it, it remains a relatively weak tactic.

This does not mean we do not support the boycott—we do. But our job is to explain that it is the power of women and our allies in the streets, and not the power of our meager purses, that is decisive.

In fact, the boycott offers an opportunity for the labor fakers and other reformist "friends of women" to show their "support" for the ERA in a way that lets them off the hook on mobilizing their ranks in action.

Electoral strategy

The deadline extension and boycott campaigns fit together in the leadership's central effort of defeating "enemies" and electing "friends" of women in the fall elections. The model, played up in the *National NOW Times,* is the campaign by Virginia NOW that helped unseat Democrat James Thompson, an outspoken opponent of the ERA of long standing, in the November 1977 elections.

The NOW leadership has widely publicized the anti-Thompson campaign both as the example for what the rest of the membership should do and to prove to the capitalist politicians that NOW has "clout."

By contrast, NOW's central leaders did little or nothing to publicize and build the first labor-led march for the ERA scheduled just two months later in Richmond, Virginia. National NOW's endorsement was never explicitly given, even though Smeal spoke at the rally.

Virginia NOW leaders concentrated their efforts on a special lobbying action held eleven days before the January 22 march. This posture is consistent with the leadership's frequently adopted stance of tolerating, but not actively building, demonstrations around the ERA, abortion rights, and other issues when local units are determined to carry them out.

The same approach lies behind their "southern strategy" outlined at the December NOW national board meeting. There the leadership discussed a proposal to involve Black women in the southern states in the campaign to win passage of the ERA.

Underneath this proposal, NOW's southern strategy, in essence, is to establish links with Black elected officials to get more Black Democrats elected to the state legislatures in the South—not the independent mobilization of Black women to fight for their rights.

This gets to the heart of one of the other important changes that should be noted. The NOW leadership has begun to talk about the need for "alliances" with labor and Black community leaders. But, this is not an alliance to mobilize the ranks of labor or the Black population. Rather, they are seeking an electoral bloc with the misleaders of the working class around a common perspective of organizing to become a "power" within the two-party system. Thus NOW leaders have stepped up their meetings and joint work with the CLUW leadership, some sections of the union bureaucracy, and some Black pro–Democratic Party organizations and individuals.

For the NOW leadership, this is one side of its efforts to project an image of building serious power blocs while at the same time using demagogy against NOW militants who have argued for a genuine alliance in action with Blacks and labor.

Minority Women's Steering Committee

The Minority Women's Steering Committee was established under pressure from the ranks of NOW, particularly women of the oppressed nationalities. After the scandalous treatment accorded these women at the Detroit conference last April, the leadership decided to establish the committee, which had been approved, in any case, by the convention.

Instead of allowing elections for the steering committee, the national NOW leadership appointed its members. This serves to keep the committee's activities strictly under the control of the national NOW board in the hopes of containing the militant Black women, Chicanas, and other Latinas in the ranks.

Nevertheless, the existence of NOW's Minority Women's Steering Committee is a contradiction for the leadership. The committee is NOW's visible commitment to involving Black women, Chicanas, Puertorriqueñas, Asian-American and Native American women in the organization. But these women will expect results from this committee.

They will see this as an opportunity to participate more fully in NOW and in its leadership bodies. The existence of the national steering committee also raises the need to set up minority women's committees and task forces in the local chapters.

Occasionally the leadership has made what appears to be shifts to the left on other issues as well. For example, after the defeat in Dade County, Florida, for gay rights last June, NOW leaders called for "action" around gay rights. They did the same thing when the Hyde amendment went into effect last August, calling for a united fight on all fronts—abortion rights, ERA, and gay rights—leading up to the IWY national conference.

But there has been a giant gap between occasional word and deed. To the extent national NOW has initiated any activities on behalf of abortion rights or gay rights, or even the ERA, it has been little but lobbying activities. For a few weeks last summer, national NOW even came out *in favor of* the reactionary Senate version of the Hyde amendment as the lesser evil. When sharp disagreements surfaced within the membership, they were forced to retract this position.

The militant rhetoric employed from time to time by the leadership is an attempt to cover their rightward political course and respond to the pressures within NOW. It reflects the contradictory character of the organization. The rhetoric serves to give credence to the leadership's official line of favoring a "multiplicity of tactics" and to refute the charge that they're using the campaign around passage of the ERA as an excuse to dump the fight on all other issues. But the reality of their orientation—and the lack of results—is becoming clearer to a layer of women in NOW who want to do whatever is necessary to win the ERA.

Red-baiting

As we predicted at the time of the last national conference, the drive to turn NOW into a different type of organization would preclude its remaining a relatively loose—though not totally democratic—group with general autonomy at the local level. The looseness of functioning inside NOW would have to be replaced with an increasingly bureaucratic method of functioning. The first step would be to try to silence those critics of the new line within NOW.

This began to be concretized at the conference itself with the red-baiting motion passed at the end of the last session against the "tactics" of SWP women in NOW. The intent of this motion was threefold: (1) to indicate that NOW was adopting a more "responsible" image in which "radicals" would be kept in line; (2) to intimidate the membership; and (3) to legitimize the second-class status of SWP members in NOW, thereby encouraging efforts to exclude SWP members from leadership positions, and hopefully drive us out of the organization [see appendix, *Militant* articles].

This red-baiting campaign was organized and led by the central national leaders of NOW, even though it was the then Philadelphia chapter president, Nada Chandler, who introduced the anti-SWP motion. Only the reaction against the red-baiting by significant numbers of NOW members convinced the leadership to mute their direct attack on SWP members in NOW at that time. What NOW leaders have done since then is to shift the red-baiting to local attacks around the country. These are promoted by national board members and frequently based on the Detroit motion, or the Los Angeles County *NOW Times* article—"SWP: A Study in Political Parasitism"—or both. In the last few months the attack on SWP members and other proponents of mass action in NOW has intensified.

A few examples indicate the pattern these attacks have followed. In Denver, where a campus-based NOW chapter began to take root, state NOW leaders responded with a red-baiting attack at a public rally, which was then covered by the media. They charged an "SWP take-over." Arlie Scott, national NOW Action vice-president, participated in the dispute on the side of the red-baiters, publicly announcing to the press that similar "problems" with the SWP had occurred in other cities. A formal grievance against that campus chapter has been filed with the state leadership in Colorado.

In Salt Lake City, the action-oriented NOW chapter has practically faded from the scene of women's liberation activity. Following the NOW Southwest Regional Conference, conservative members in the chapter launched a red-baiting campaign against the then-chapter president, Kay Sedam, hoping to drive her out of the chapter. These red-baiters openly explained that they were collaborating with national board members in California and Washington, D.C.

NOW members in New Orleans succeeded in revitalizing their chapter and were immediately faced with charges of an SWP "take-over" and demands by conservative NOW leaders in a nearby chapter that their charter be revoked. National NOW officers refused New Orleans NOW's request for help in preserving their chapter. Only the strong stand against exclusion taken by Louisiana state NOW leaders helped to defuse the situation. But many serious members left the New Orleans chapter after the long and frustrating fight.

Campus NOW chapters are beginning to face the same discrimination. The coordinator of the NOW Northeast Region High School and College Women's Outreach Committee reported at their January 7, 1978, meeting that newly formed campus chapters in places like Boston; Amherst, Massachusetts; San Diego; and Chicago were being denied charters for "political reasons." The explanation for refusing to convene these chapters given during informal discussions was the fear of NOW state presidents that SWP members were participating in them.

At that meeting, the regional campus committee voted to request that the national NOW board prepare convenors' kits for every campus chapter that requests one. They also urged the board to establish a clear national policy on chartering campus chapters at its February meeting.

The most serious attempt to date to exclude militants from NOW has been in Philadelphia, where seven of the nine chapter officers resigned and then began a vicious slander campaign in the media. They charged SWP members with disrupting the chapter through "too much discussion" in which they raised proposals for mass actions.

What makes the Philadelphia case so important is that the national NOW board decided to intervene openly, by setting up a fact-finding committee over which the local membership had no control. This committee was charged with making recommendations on guidelines that will no doubt aim to further restrict democracy in NOW. At its February meeting, the NOW national board appointed a new grievance committee that is charged with reporting it's findings on the Philadelphia case to a special national board meeting in March.

These few examples strongly indicate that the national NOW leadership, while not publicly leading the red-baiting attacks, has been complicit in them and actually organized them behind the scenes. National NOW leaders have avoided openly calling for the expulsion of SWP members. Rather, their tactic is to implement the anti-SWP motion, passed in Detroit, by raising the specter of the "SWP problem" to isolate anyone who agrees with ideas and proposals for a political course different from that of the national NOW leadership. The Philadelphia events also show that NOW leaders are not above destroying chapters in order to kill debate and opposition to their line.

The red-baiting has demoralized some of the best NOW activists in Philadelphia and hurt the organization as a whole. But at the same time, a layer of NOW members in the chapter are willing to fight these undemocratic moves. This again indicates the contradictory character of NOW and that the leadership's efforts to totally destroy internal democracy will continue to meet resistance. Organizing that support forces the national leadership to deescalate its attacks as it has done by dissolving the special Philadelphia committee into a grievance committee.

Meaning of NOW's turn

As we explained after the April conference, the process under way in NOW—which encompasses its ERA strategy, its developing ties with the liberal misleaderships in the Black and labor movements, its shoulder-rubbing with capitalist politicians in Washington, D.C.—is designed to housebreak the women's movement. The ruling class must create an authoritative leadership it can rely on to dominate the movement and undercut organized resistance by women to the attacks on their rights. That's why the bourgeois media hailed the election of NOW President Eleanor Smeal, who brags about "never having worked for a salary" in her life. The *Boston Globe, Christian Science Monitor,* and the *New York Times* hailed this change in NOW's image. As the *Times* editors put it after the April conference, the women's movement was "learning, as the civil rights movement did before it, that beyond the heady early victories lies the hard-scrabble of institutional reality."

The ruling-class parties, the Democrats and Republicans, also welcomed this new leadership. Smeal's Rose Garden conversation with President Carter, her White House conferences with his administrative aides, and the organized participation of NOW chapter leaderships in the election campaigns of "pro-ERA" politicians exemplify their new working relationship as part of the two-party system. NOW leaders are becoming an acceptable part of the "team."

This is best exemplified in their role at the National Women's Conference in Houston. Together with Democratic and some Republican Party leaders, NOW officials organized to control the conference through the pro-plan caucus.

Using the presence of a small minority of right-wing delegates as a justification for limiting democratic discussion, the pro-plan caucus helped to ram through the plan with little or no debate and with a few orchestrated changes in its wording. Changes in the plank on minority women's rights were the one exception. Absolutely no discussion took place on the government's responsibility for the attacks on women's rights.

In their public statements following the Houston conference, NOW leaders said they, of course, had been in favor of a more democratic conference—even though that sentiment apparently didn't guide their actions. NOW emerged from the IWY conference with even greater authority as part of the recognized leadership in today's women's movement.

NOW's attraction

In her January plenum report last year, Cindy Jaquith pointed out, "Basically NOW is an organization that reflects the 1960s radicalization. Its policies can be influenced, and many feminists in NOW are looking for a political perspective that shows the way forward."

This remains true in NOW today. The organization is still full of contradictions. But the leadership continues to move toward tightening up, limiting freedom of action and discussion, pressing to turn NOW into an organization in the women's movement more like the NAACP or Urban League. It's a process that is still evolving, with much resistance. On the chapter level, it is very uneven and opportunities for discussing and organizing visible activities still exist in many places. The leadership still responds to pressures within the organization.

Objectively, conditions for women are getting worse and the need for a discussion on strategy remains urgent. Clarifying "Which way forward?" and building the women's liberation movement are totally intertwined.

What kind of discussion is possible in NOW in coming months?

Nationally, NOW's authority is increasing, and it is attracting women by the thousands. NOW reports a current membership of 70,000 and more than 770 chapters. Many new NOW members are concerned about the cutoff of federal funds for abortions, forced sterilization, the threat to jobs and education.

Besides NOW, there is no other national organization that women activists are joining in significant numbers. So NOW remains the only national organization in which the broad discussion necessary to move the women's movement forward can really occur.

When this discussion began, it was clear that there would be no quick resolution of the issues. What was necessary was to begin discussing who was responsible for the attacks on women's rights, and what to do to organize an effective response. Now it's important to ask: Where does this discussion stand today? *What has been accomplished?*

We participated in this debate on the alternative strategy for the women's movement prior to the last NOW national conference. Eighty NOW members, including some who also belonged to the SWP, signed the resolution on defending women's rights that was presented to the April conference. At the conference more than 200 NOW members participated in a caucus around the Defending Women's Rights platform.

After the conference, we as NOW members participated in projects in local chapters, won respect for the work we did in helping to organize activities around the resolution perspective, and gained acceptance in NOW as feminists and activists. The perspective we advocated has also influenced some local NOW chapters to sponsor activities and work jointly with other groups. The discussion started in Detroit has been continued through the publication of the monthly, *Defending Women's Rights Newsletter*.

The perspective for education and action that we advanced has been borne out on numerous occasions. The June attacks on abortion rights prompted many NOW chapters to initiate or co-sponsor picket lines and news conferences. Some NOW chapters also participated in abortion actions last fall protesting the appearances of U.S. Representative Henry Hyde; Health, Education and Welfare Secretary Joseph Califano; and President Carter. These actions helped to force national NOW to change its initial position of support to the Senate's proposed abortion restrictions. A number of NOW chapters also organized abortion rights actions this January 22—the fifth anniversary of the 1973 abortion legalization decision.

In California new activists were attracted to NOW gatherings during the lively debate around the need for guidelines to curb sterilization abuse. While NOW members supporting the guidelines were unable to win a majority of the California organization, the debate helped to convince a section of the leadership of the need to support the guidelines, as well as to win over and involve many activists in that important struggle.

Campus women have been won to NOW, despite the leadership's traditional lack of attention to the campuses. The potential militancy of student feminists is not lost on the NOW leadership. These women would have a big impact on NOW, especially the current perspectives discussions unfolding in the organization.

In addition to the growing interest in NOW among campus women, minority women's committees in some NOW chapters have encouraged a growing number of Black women and Chicanas to begin to attend NOW meetings and to join NOW.

Newsletter initiated

At last summer's regional NOW conferences, informal discussions with NOW members—many of whom had not attended the April conference—helped to lay the basis for publishing the *Defending Women's Rights Newsletter*. The newsletter has been circulated to many activists in the women's movement. The ease with which it can be sold has proved that it is the best vehicle for reaching out to and staying in touch nationally with NOW members who support the perspective it puts forward.

Last summer the newsletter called for actions in

response to attacks on abortion rights, and it then reported on the actions that were held. It explained the importance of the International Women's Year national conference and encouraged all women to attend and participate. Later, the newsletter analyzed the impact of the conference and pointed to the next steps forward for the women's movement.

Articles in the newsletter have explained the meaning of the pro-*Bakke* ruling for equal educational and employment opportunities for women. The articles called on the women's movement to get involved in the local anti-*Bakke* actions and the march on Washington, D.C., April 15.

The newsletter has served to maintain contact with those NOW members who participated in the campaign both before and at the April national NOW conference, and to reach new NOW members as they became interested in the strategy discussion.

The *National NOW Times* has called on the NOW membership to step up letter writing and lobbying to "pressure" politicians. In contrast, the *Defending Women's Rights Newsletter* has called on feminists to depend on themselves to make gains by organizing their collective power together with their allies. Currently, more than 700 women subscribe to the *Defending Women's Rights Newsletter*—an important indicator of the impact of these ideas in NOW and on the women's movement in general.

Membership's expectations

Most NOW members do not understand that the NOW leadership's present course is counterposed to building an independent women's movement. Probably most members support both actions called to defend women's rights and proposals to get involved in campaigns for "pro-ERA" capitalist politicians. For them, NOW's electoral orientation is "just another tactic" to win ratification. It has no bearing on NOW's political independence.

For example, the Ohio state NOW conference voted last December to make three campaigns their main activities this year: (1) an intensive letter-writing and lobbying effort for the ERA extension campaign; (2) raising funds to hire a full-time lobbyist in the state capitol; and (3) support to a Democratic Party woman running for Congress. Just as enthusiastically, NOW members passed a resolution calling for a statewide abortion rights rally. The same political confusion marked the activities of Indiana NOW members before the ERA was ratified there in January 1977.

Since the defeats for the ERA in the South Carolina legislature and in committee in the Virginia legislature, NOW leaders have called a "state of emergency" for the ERA. They hope to drive through their electoral strategy by creating a crisis atmosphere that will cloud the real thrust and ineffectiveness of this strategy. They also hope to stampede the membership to comply with their political plan by projecting a panic over the ERA and excluding activity on all other issues.

Their ERA Strike Force is designed to facilitate the orientation announced in their latest mailing. A new and separate organization called NOW Political Action Committee has been set up, in order to legally support their friends in the Democratic and Republican parties without jeopardizing NOW's tax-exempt status.

The ERA Strike Force moves around showing the film *How We Got the Vote* and trying to convince women to use the vote to put their "friends" in office. Dianne Feeley's article in the March 1978 issue of the *International Socialist Review* explains the class-struggle methods that were used in the suffrage movement to win the vote—which, of course, leads one to the opposite conclusions from those drawn by the NOW leadership.

The national strike force will undoubtedly be used increasingly elsewhere, as it has been in Arizona, to reverse chapter decisions that conflict with election campaign work.

NOW's national policy is to support "pro-ERA" capitalist candidates regardless of their positions on other issues. And more and more the leadership is trying to make agreement with its tactics and orientations—instead of support to feminist goals—the basis for membership in NOW. The idea is beginning to be raised that to question the leadership is somehow not loyal to NOW. As these restrictions bear down on NOW members without the leadership delivering some victories, more NOW members will begin to see that the independent strategy posed at the last national conference is all the more urgent. As the national leadership's resistance grows to local planning and priorities in the chapters, other NOW members will be encouraged to fight for democracy in NOW.

Next stage of discussion

The next national NOW conference is scheduled for October 6–8 in Washington, D.C. It offers an important opportunity to discuss broadly the political ideas needed as a basis for defending and extending women's rights.

We have no interest in a "power struggle" or in taking over positions in NOW. What NOW members who oppose subordinating the women's movement to the capitalist politicians must do is continue to clarify what's happening in the offensive to roll back the gains women have won, to explain why it's happening, help women understand how to fight back effectively, and win the maximum number of women—whether it's one, two, five, or ten—to support a perspective that can move the women's movement forward. This was important at the beginning of the discussion, and it continues to be what must be done today.

Members of the Socialist Workers Party and Young Socialist Alliance joined with other NOW members at the 1977 NOW national conference to put forward the Defending Women's Rights resolution. The key planks of that program were the following: (1) the need for NOW to recognize the attacks on women's rights on many fronts; (2) to reach out to the most immediate victims—working-class women, mostly Black women, Chicanas, Puertorriqueñas, and young women; (3) to mobilize women in coalitions with their allies in the labor movement and the communities of the oppressed nationalities in a campaign of education and action; and (4) to organize to build an independent women's liberation movement free from the control of or dependence on the politicians in the Democratic and Republican parties.

These same elements are key to the alternative strategy that must be posed today. But the question of dependence on Democrats and Republicans will have to be a major focus of the discussion from the beginning. In addition, the right to have a free, open exchange of ideas in NOW will have to be fought for.

NOW members must have the guaranteed right to express their political views, whether they are the same or different from those of the leadership. If not, it will be impossible for NOW's membership to develop a course of action that can build NOW and the women's movement.

NOW's failure to mobilize around and consistently fight for abortion rights, the ERA, against sterilization abuse, and the other attacks facing women will also be focuses of this discussion. But in each case, the root of the problem lies in the *overall* strategy proposed by the leadership. In order to effectively explain what is wrong with this strategy, a clear alternative on how to build the feminist movement must be put forward to clarify the two perspectives open to NOW.

This was done effectively last year through the general resolution on defending women's rights. Its supporters also introduced other resolutions on specific related issues, including women of oppressed nationalities, campus women, abortion, the ERA, and others.

This year, again, a resolution along the lines of the Defending Women's Rights perspective could be a focus to continue and deepen the discussion on strategy leading up to and at the NOW convention.

Because of the wide support for nonexclusion in NOW—support that extends to women who disagree with the alternative perspective—NOW members have already begun to organize a campaign around democratic norms, and put forward resolutions on this question. An example of this is the Milwaukee NOW chapter's campaign to get fifty NOW chapters to endorse an amendment to the national by-laws specifying that no woman may be excluded from membership because of political affiliation.

A clear resolution would make it possible for individual NOW leaders and activists to discuss the questions of strategy in a more focused way. NOW chapter program meetings could take up issues that are related to the perspective needed to defend and extend women's rights. The NOW regional conferences coming up in April provide an initial opportunity to hear what NOW members think about the perspective for an independent, action-oriented women's movement in light of the developments of the last year. Draft resolutions can be discussed more broadly. Workshop discussion sessions and hospitality gatherings at these conferences will offer an opportunity to win initial support, in the same way meetings at regional conferences last summer won support for the Defending Women's Rights perspective.

The *Defending Women's Rights Newsletter* will continue to be one of the most important vehicles for exchanging views on the important issues facing NOW. For seven months the newsletter has been a forum for discussing how to counter the government offensive against women's rights. Its national circulation and subscription base mean that it will be able to play a role in promoting a real discussion in NOW.

At the same time, informal discussions with individual NOW members, within local chapters and at regional conferences, are important in finding out what people think and encouraging them to attend the national NOW convention.

New national officers will not be elected at this convention. Therefore, much of the conference will certainly be oriented toward the final drive in the November elections. A full, open, democratic debate on strategy will not be uppermost in the priorities of the national leadership.

One thing they will certainly use to try to prevent such a discussion is red-baiting of SWP members and other advocates of mass action. Opposition to these attacks will have to be organized to ensure that the democratic right to hear every viewpoint and express it freely is projected prominently at the national conference.

We have had some important experiences that show the support in the membership for democracy in NOW and opposition to discrimination on the basis of political affiliation. One is the significant opposition to the anti-SWP motion passed at last year's national conference. Another is the number of chapter, state, and regional NOW meetings that have recently amended their by-laws to bar discrimination against NOW members on the basis of "political affiliation" and voted to support a similar change in the national by-laws.

The opportunity to win support among NOW members for independent political action will continue to exist side by side with the national NOW leadership's drive to impose their line on the organization.

It's important always to keep in mind that our goal is not to "expose" the NOW leadership, but to defend women's rights. Whenever there is any opportunity to move forward in that direction, we're the first to respond enthusiastically.

Scope of struggle for women's rights

It will take nothing less than a massive women's movement to regain abortion rights for *all* women. The ERA will be ratified only if a powerful independent women's movement exists. Maternity benefits for pregnant workers, affirmative action in jobs and education, government-funded child-care centers, dramatic reduction in sterilization abuse—these and other changes in the daily living conditions of women require organizing those women ready to struggle around a program that mobilizes women and their allies in the working class in action. Building an independent movement requires developing a leadership in the women's liberation movement prepared to put no other interest ahead of winning gains for women and determined to fight uncompromisingly for those gains.

These are the stakes involved in accomplishing the tasks that have been posed by the government's antiwoman drive. The ruling class is trying to establish the leadership it needs in the women's movement, trying to stifle the growth and militancy of the movement. The discussion leading up to the next national NOW conference is an opportunity to further clarify how a pro–Democratic Party orientation is a roadblock that will only continue to cripple the women's movement in the face of the government's offensive. It is also an opportunity to extend the progress already made in winning support for the kind of program that can develop and promote an independent orientation in the women's liberation movement.

What is needed is to assemble in the women's movement exactly what the coal miners represent today in the labor movement—a core of determined fighters, who are willing to place their own self-interests ahead of any concern for approval from the employers or the capitalist politicians. We want to help open the road to that development in the women's movement.

The ferment of ideas in the women's movement is precisely what has led many activists in NOW to socialist conclusions, and, in some cases, to join the socialist movement. This discussion also helps to attract activists in the broader women's movement into NOW.

Other women's groups

In the coming months we also must continue, and in some cases step up, work we've been doing to build the women's movement outside of NOW. Over the past year we have carried out activities with coalitions that included organizations such as Planned Parenthood, American Civil Liberties Union, some state affiliates of the National Abortion Rights Action League, and lesbian feminist groups, around the ERA, abortion rights, and sterilization abuse in such cities as Chicago, San Francisco, Baltimore, Portland, and New York.

These successful coalition activities have played an indispensable role in setting the practical example of how to organize broadly to win women's demands. Even where NOW has not responded favorably to such coalition activities, the pressure from such forces and activities was a crucial part of the debate inside NOW. The actions provided concrete, positive examples of how coalitions must be used to mobilize women and their supporters.

The work of other women's rights groups helps to encourage NOW leaders to support actions they do not initiate. This in turn brings out larger numbers of women's rights supporters and attracts more activists to the movement and to NOW.

Another important aspect of working in the women's movement is encouraging the organization of Black women and Latina groups. The growth of such groups in the last year has been especially noticeable.

These women represent some of the more militant forces—those who have the greatest stake in the development of a strong, independent women's movement, and the greatest stake in the fight against the government's anti–working class, antiwoman drive. Many will support actions demanding child care, employment opportunities, abortion rights, and an end to sterilization abuse. This makes it essential to convince them to join NOW, and help build it as an organization that is attractive to other women of oppressed nationalities. Their involvement generally helps to cut across NOW's class-collaborationist orientation and aids in bringing more working-class women into NOW and the women's movement as a whole.

NOW's Minority Women's Committee has announced a number of spring conferences. We as NOW members will want to encourage these women to join NOW and help build and participate in these conferences when they are scheduled.

The work we do with Black women and Latina groups helps to underscore the spread of feminism. It helps to attract other women from the communities of the oppressed nationalities to actions around women's issues. Together with our work in the labor movement especially, it helps to lay the foundations for the development of national Black, Chicana, and Puertorriqueña feminist organizations that are missing today.

We've seen a similar growth of interest in the women's movement among organized working women. This has focused especially on the issues of affirmative action and the ERA. Examples of this are the interest of the delegates at the CLUW convention last fall in discussing the questions of affirmative action and the *Bakke* case, and the USWA District 31 women's conference this winter and the resolution supporting the Equal Rights Amendment passed there. Black women in the Virginia Amalgamated Meat Cutters played the key role in initiating and building the sizable pro-ERA labor demonstration in Richmond January 22. That action is an example we can point to in our discussions with co-workers on the job of the kind of labor support for women's rights that is needed to win gains for women.

The ferment and growth of new formations in the women's movement opens up more opportunities to meet and have discussions with feminists in many groups. We should continue to take advantage of these opportunities and step up our participation wherever and whenever it is possible to do so.

The *Militant* will continue to play an important role in educating on the roots of women's oppression, the state of the leadership in the women's movement, and the ruling-class attacks on women's rights. It will help to organize women to fight back. Our election campaigns and our forums continue to be vital tools for explaining how feminists should participate in the electoral arena by putting forward the working-class alternative to the traitors in the two capitalist parties.

There is no question that the decision we have

made at this plenum to speed up the process of getting the majority of the party—including female members, of course—into industry and in industrial unions will have an important and positive impact on all our women's liberation activity.

We expect that the steps we've decided upon will enable us to take full advantage of new openings and opportunities for women's liberation activities in the organized labor movement. By getting more members into steel, auto, rail, and other industrial jobs and unions, we'll not only be in a better position to talk socialism to many more workers. We'll also be in a better position to talk feminism with many more working-class women, and win them to a fighting, independent women's movement and to NOW, as well as to our party.

This view of our work helps to show that the changes we are making are *not* in contradiction to stepping up our work to build NOW. On the contrary, they are totally complementary.

The fundamental problem in the women's movement today remains that of posing and getting support for a strategy necessary to counter and beat back the challenges to women's rights. This is the same problem that confronts our class as a whole: to chart an independent course to fight back as the capitalists and their politicians strive to tighten the screws. The discussions we will have on the job with our co-workers are the same kinds of discussions that are taking place in NOW.

The two counterposed perspectives in NOW must be debated out with the purpose of gaining support for a winning strategy and convincing women in NOW and in the women's movement as a whole to fight to establish that perspective to advance the struggle for women's liberation. It's a *political* battle that cannot be avoided. It's one that would have to be fought out in the long run, regardless of which organization is in the leadership of the women's movement.

Our present orientation of getting a majority of the party into industry will enable us to take the next important steps in this process. As industrial workers, we will be able to reach out to and involve those forces that we believe must become the leadership in the working class and in the independent struggles and organizations of its allies, including the women's movement.

The interrelated process can only enhance the discussion in NOW. The stumbling block presented for the women's movement by the NOW leaders' political reliance on the ruling class can only be overcome in the long run if it is possible to bring the power of working-class forces to bear around a class-struggle program.

Our participation in the women's movement, and our greater involvement in the industrial work force, will lay a solid foundation for the next stage of building the politically independent women's movement that is needed. The discussion of perspectives in NOW is crucial. It is taking place in the context of more, not fewer, attacks on women's rights and at a time when more women will be looking for answers.

Summary

As Cindy [Jaquith] mentioned, and as we know from our experiences in working to build NOW, opportunities for actions and discussion vary widely. The real question we have to ask ourselves is whether there is some alternative. Is there some better way to build the women's liberation movement, to gain political clarification, to help get actions going on a national or a regional level?

When you pose that question, I think you have to come to the conclusion that at this particular time there is no better way to defend women's rights.

There are some other ways to build the women's movement on a local level. In a number of cities from time to time, viable action coalitions emerge around one or another issue. We build them and help them go as far as they can. One example was the action coalition to build the abortion rights demonstration in New York last fall when Califano came to town. In a number of places there are coalitions around March 8 activity, and so forth. These coalitions usually come together around a single action and then dissolve.

Any ongoing coalition like that around the ERA in Illinois is unusual. In fact, I don't know of any other like it.

When those kinds of actions come along, we have to build them, build the coalitions, see how far they can develop. Very active, political women are involved in them; we have very good political discussions in them. We can help to organize good actions that serve as an example of what should be done. This is an important part of building NOW, as well.

But we always come back to the same contradiction. Even the best of the local coalitions, like the one in Illinois, are isolated. Starting from there it's very hard to pose on a national level the question of what strategy for the women's movement, how do we move forward, how do we mobilize women to defend their rights.

And this kind of a discussion must take place on a *national* level. That's what the real problem is.

The truth of the matter is that the only opposition anywhere to this political derailment of the women's movement is what we're doing to help counter it, to clarify it, to force a discussion about it, to raise an alternative perspective. Even in all the action coalitions and campus organizations and other groups, there are few women who understand that the issue is the question of class independence. The same issue is posed in the women's movement, in the Black movement, in the labor movement. It's the question of leadership.

We have gained a lot of valuable experience in our work to build the women's movement over the last year. We can also see from the discussion today some of the opportunities we have, the limitations, and the input that we're having in the women's movement.

The discussion prior to the last national NOW conference turned out to be very rich, taking up all types of questions, from the role of Black women, to what is the program of the women's movement and what kind of actions are needed. This time the discussion will be even richer. The whole question of independent political action will be posed much more sharply and explicitly. It is a question that miners have to think about; it is a question that people in the steel union have to think about; the Black movement has to think about it, and so on. It will become a much bigger part of the discussion in the women's movement in the next months, and it is going to be a very good discussion. We will be able to convince women that the positions of the party and the YSA are correct.

Finally, it's important to return to the basic decisions we have made at this plenum to get the majority of our members into industry as rapidly as possible.

As we raised in the report, and as a number of comrades took up in the discussion, this will have a real impact on our women's liberation work. We will be in a position to involve our co-workers in all kinds of activities, including joining NOW. We will be in a better position to raise the social issues posed by the women's liberation movement inside the unions and win labor support for women's demands. It will be easier to demonstrate concretely the interrelationship between the struggle for women's liberation and the needs of the working class. And it is from the working class that the future leadership of the women's movement must come if we are to win our liberation.

So we're taking a big step forward with this plenum. The process will have to be consciously led in relation to our work to build the women's movement. It is not counterposed to our task of trying to discuss and clarify a national perspective that would enable the women's movement to mobilize its forces and bring the full weight of ourselves and our allies to bear. On the contrary, it will strengthen the contributions we can make to this discussion. It will enable us to do a better job of building NOW, and CLUW, and action coalitions, and campus groups, and other women's organizations. It will mean an effective increase in our work to build the women's movement.

Appendix: April 1977 national NOW conference

2,000 FEMINISTS DEBATE STRATEGY FOR MOVEMENT
Reprinted from the 'Militant,' May 6, 1977

By Nancy Cole

DETROIT—Nearly 2,000 women gathered here April 21–24 for the annual conference of the National Organization for Women. The conference celebrated NOW's tenth anniversary, and a debate over political perspectives for the second decade worked its way to the surface.

The first scheduled event was a march and rally of 1,000 in pouring rain to demand ratification of the Equal Rights Amendment. The women were angry about the latest ERA defeats, and the protest demonstrated a willingness on their part to do something about the assault on their right to equality.

Many members of NOW had come to the conference concerned that victories for women won during NOW's first decade—the right to legal abortions, affirmative action in hiring and promotions, childcare programs—were in danger of being lost.

Many of the 770 delegates and the 1,200 members (who had speaking but not voting rights) were in Detroit to discuss these problems, to exchange ideas, and to decide on a course to turn the tide against the enemies of women's rights.

These women succeeded in making their voices heard, initiating a discussion on how to respond to the dangers facing NOW and the women's movement.

Avoid scrutiny

Other members of NOW, unfortunately, had a different kind of conference in mind. The new national leadership wanted to *prevent* a full discussion of political perspectives and to avoid any close scrutiny of their proposals for action.

One method used by newly elected President Eleanor Smeal and others was to stress the theme of "unity" within NOW over a strategy to win the Equal Rights Amendment. Those who differed with that strategy could then be branded disrupters, uninterested in building NOW and in winning the ERA.

On the first day of the conference, before any political discussion had taken place, outgoing President Karen DeCrow told reporters that "every NOW member agrees on political action." She went on to describe that action, which included working to elect "pro-ERA" Democrats in 1978, urging President Carter to set an ERA blitz campaign, and launching an economic boycott of unratified states.

As early as February, more than eighty women from around the country had submitted a resolution for discussion at the conference that proposed a road for NOW in stark contrast to the one outlined by DeCrow.

Called "Defending Women's Rights in the Second Decade," this resolution would have NOW launch a drive, independent of the Democratic and Republican parties, to counter the right-wing attacks on women's rights with a massive educational and action campaign.

In order to cloud discussion of this perspective, opponents of the resolution branded it a Socialist Workers Party resolution. Supporters of this independent perspective were dubbed "dupes" of the SWP.

Leaders of NOW charged the SWP had brought a "hidden agenda" to the conference. This frenzied campaign to discredit the ideas supported by members of the SWP along with many other women at the conference finally erupted in a last-minute, hysterical redbaiting motion. The motion, which passed, "protested" the SWP's attempts to "use" NOW to bring the SWP's "agenda" before the public.

'Hidden agenda'

But who had the "hidden agenda"? Was it the women who came to the conference urging a full, open debate over NOW's future course? Or was it the NOW leaders who wanted to use the meeting to make official their plans to transform NOW into a "force" within the Democratic party?

Supporters of the resolution on Defending Women's Rights openly circulated their proposal. It was reported on and reprinted in several major women's publications, including *Majority Report* and *Off Our Backs*. Numerous NOW chapters had discussed it prior to the conference.

A caucus formed to support the resolution held daily meetings open to all conference participants. More than 250 women attended.

Members of the caucus took the floor during workshops and plenaries, explained their perspective, and urged those who disagreed to bring the debate into the open. The resolution, however, never officially reached the floor for discussion.

The conference agenda was set up to avoid such a debate. The campaigning and election of officers took up the bulk of plenary sessions. Discussion on resolutions for the coming year's *activities* was relegated to the very last four hours of the conference, on Sunday afternoon.

To many women this seemed backwards. The logical order—and that most productive and democratic—would be for the political discussion and decisions on priorities for the coming year to precede the elections.

Supporters of the Defending Women's Rights caucus—and participants in the Minority Women workshop, abortion rights workshop, and others—urged remedying this somewhat. They requested that a two-hour slot be inserted in the agenda on Saturday for an initial discussion of the resolutions.

"Yesterday at a press conference, Karen DeCrow said there was unity in NOW," Clare Fraenzl said in arguing for the agenda adjustment. Fraenzl, vice-president for liaison of the Philadelphia chapter, was an initiator along with Rhonda Rutherford of the Defending Women's Rights resolution.

"Well, I think there is unity in terms of our determination to build NOW and to make it grow," she continued. "But I think in terms of the strategy we have been using, there is a great deal of discussion that must come out on the floor.

"Karen DeCrow said today that it is not our fault that the ERA was not passed. But I would maintain that it is our *default*.... I think we need to discuss this out in detail and have these issues presented to the membership before we can have any decision on candidates."

The proposal to amend the agenda was defeated.

Two resolutions constituted the program of the NOW leadership. They were a proposal to set up a National ERA Strike Force, and a proposal to launch a national Political Action Committee.

The strike force, a small committee appointed by and headed by the NOW president, would be "charged with planning overall strategy" at all levels of the organization to win the ERA.

The Political Action Committee would collect contributions and deliver them to the candidates of NOW's choice.

"There is no way we're going to get the ERA without changing the composition of state legislatures," national board member Toni Carabillo said under discussion of the PAC proposal.

Unlike other votes during the plenaries—when about 75 percent of delegates voted with the leadership—the vote on the PAC proposal was close. The chairperson called for a standing vote before declaring the resolution passed.

As the Defending Women's Rights resolution gained wider circulation and became a topic of discussion in more workshops, the NOW leaders demagogically stepped up their claims to favor a "multiplicity of tactics."

Yet in a workshop on the ERA, Smeal declared she would "work against" a resolution submitted by New York City delegate Dianne Feeley. That proposal urged NOW to call a demonstration for some date in the fall to protest all the attacks on women's rights.

Smeal and others charged that supporters of a massive, independent women's movement favored only one tactic to the exclusion of all others. Members of the Defending Women's Rights caucus took every opportunity to explain to the entire conference that the debate was not over one tactic versus many—but rather, over the *strategy* for winning women's rights.

'Militancy'

By the time Smeal gave her acceptance speech on Sunday, she was promising an ERA campaign that would include "high visibility and militancy."

But the discussion at the conference and the methods employed by the leadership here proved this to be rhetoric.

To organize a campaign of "high visibility and militancy," NOW would have to turn to the women most willing to be visible and militant. These are the women with the most to lose in the current war against women's rights—Black, Puerto Rican, Chicana, and other working-class women.

To reach these women, NOW would have to place high priority on their needs; it would have to defend their rights, including abortion, affirmative-action programs, child care, and protection against sterilization abuse.

Rather than declare NOW's desire to recruit these women in massive numbers during the next year, Smeal chose to emphasize a campaign to reach out to "homemakers."

The message of this focus is clear: NOW leaders intend to maintain the image of the group as a white, middle-class movement.

The NOW leaders failed to address any issues except the ERA, and they actually stifled discussion on the other issues of vital concern to Black and other working women.

A conference resolutions committee "prioritized" resolutions in the order they were to be discussed. Some resolutions were prioritized right out of existence.

A resolution from NOW members in Minneapolis was declared a "local matter" and referred to the national board. The resolution sought reversal of a racist Twin Cities NOW report charging that state affirmative-action programs profited Black men at the expense of women.

Another resolution, from California NOW members, asked the conference to reaffirm NOW's stand against forced sterilization and to go on record in support of guidelines to curb sterilization abuse. The proposal was intended to counter a California state board stand *against* such guidelines in that state.

This resolution was omitted from the list of proposals to be discussed, with no explanation given.

The first category of resolutions was the ERA. Of seven resolutions, the ERA Strike Force proposal was first, the resolution on Defending Women's Rights, last.

The entire time allotment for all seven was thirty minutes. Needless to say, only the first resolution—the strike force—was voted on. It passed.

A resolution on Women of the Oppressed Nationalities was also omitted from the resolutions committee list. This resolution had been endorsed by the Minority Women workshop, which met several times during the conference.

The proposal urged NOW to organize activities that could reach out to and recruit Black, Chicana, Puerto Rican, Native American, and Asian women.

Participants in the Minority Women workshop demanded that this proposal be put on the plenary floor for discussion. This motion was passed.

The resolution as amended called for concrete activities as well as a national committee on minority women to help carry out these actions.

Opponents of the resolution, who did not want to come out and openly oppose a campaign to recruit Black women, sought to disguise their objections. Jeane Bendorff, California state coordinator of NOW, moved to separate the action part of the resolution from the proposal to establish a committee.

The rest of the scheduled half-hour discussion was taken up with parliamentary filibustering. Delegates then voted up the committee proposal and defeated the proposals for action.

Not one person had expressed her objections to the defeated resolution.

To the outrage of many delegates, opponents even applauded and cheered this insulting vote against the Black and Latina members of NOW.

Pat Wright, a Black NOW member from Brooklyn, went to the microphone. "What this conference has just done here in front of the press is a scandal for NOW," she said.

"By voting against this resolution, we have hurt NOW's ability to reach out to Black, Puerto Rican, and Chicana women."

Rumors

Throughout the conference, rumors circulated about threatened "disruptions" by members of the Socialist Workers Party.

The leading role played by Black, Chicana, and

Puerto Rican women in bringing to the fore issues of concern to the most exploited women was attributed to a "take-over" of the Minority Women workshop by "militant" Black SWP members.

There was even an insidious effort to incite white NOW members against Black and Latina women. As the resolution on Women of the Oppressed Nationalities was defeated, rumors of a "riot" swept the plenary. Security guards were obviously alerted and an unusually large number milled in the hallway.

This atmosphere was bolstered by a slanderous article in the Los Angeles County NOW Times called "SWP: A Study in Political Parasitism." It was widely distributed to those attending the conference.

This attack backfired right from the start.

At the first meeting of the Defending Women's Rights caucus on Friday night, Esther Kaw, NOW national vice-president for public relations, stormed to the front of the room.

She explained that she had come to the conference "fully prepared to vote against this resolution" on Defending Women's Rights. But after reading the piece of "yellow journalism" in the *NOW Times,* she decided to support the resolution.

"I'm not a member of the Socialist Workers Party," she said. "I'm not going to ever be. . . . But I don't think this is the way to handle disagreements."

Kaw went on to refute the charge that the SWP was "using" Black, Chicana, and other women of oppressed nationalities.

"I'm going to tell you. I'm Chicana, and it ain't all that easy to use me!"

At the scheduled adjournment time, supporters of the Defending Women's Rights resolution and the resolution on Women of the Oppressed Nationalities held a brief caucus meeting to discuss their next steps in carrying forward this discussion in NOW chapters across the country.

After these women left the conference hall, Smeal took the microphone to call the press into the hall for an important announcement.

Near hysteria

Women attending the caucus meeting learned of this and immediately returned to the hall, where an atmosphere of near hysteria prevailed. Valerie Coffee, a Black woman who is co-coordinator of Trenton, New Jersey, NOW, was at the microphone, objecting to a news conference allegedly called by the Minority Women workshop to denounce NOW as "racist."

"I think it's about time the Socialist Workers Party stopped using the issue of minority rights as a tool to recruit people," she said.

But no "news conference" had ever been scheduled by the Minority Women workshop. In fact, no one seemed to know how this mysterious rumor originated.

Esther Kaw demanded the floor to refute the rumor. "Speaking for the Minority Women workshop, I can tell you that such a news conference was never called," she said.

Several reporters also asked for the floor to confirm that they were never contacted about such a news conference.

No one from the Minority Women workshop could be found to authenticate the news conference story. But Black and Latina women attempting to *refute* the myth were abruptly cut off when they demanded the floor and were shouted down by other delegates.

In the heated atmosphere clearly sustained by the podium, Nada Chandler, president of Philadelphia NOW, placed a red-baiting motion on the floor. The motion charged that the SWP was trying to "use" NOW and to "exploit the feminist movement."

Dianne Feeley, a longtime leader of the New York NOW and a member of the SWP, took the floor, stating, "This motion is a red-baiting tactic that is no different from lesbian-baiting or any other form of witch-hunting in NOW. It is the same tactic that has been used against the Black movement, the suffrage movement, the labor movement. We must reject it and declare that NOW is open to all women, regardless of their political affiliation."

'Enemies' tactic'

Several other members of the Socialist Workers Party tried to get the floor to respond to the outrageous motion. The chair ruled them out of order. The red-baiting motion passed. Then the conference was adjourned.

Angered by the introduction of McCarthyism into NOW, more than 100 NOW members met at the back of the hall to protest this attack on democracy in their organization.

"Red-baiting is the tactic of our enemies, a well-known trick of the FBI," said one delegate.

The meeting drew up a petition stating, "We are opposed to the resolution against the SWP, which is also a resolution against NOW. NOW should be open to all women regardless of their political persuasions."

One hundred twelve NOW members had signed the statement by the next morning, when the petition was presented to a meeting of the NOW National Board.

At the board meeting, Lois Reckitt, an eastern regional coordinator of NOW, introduced a motion to reaffirm that NOW is open to all women and does not discriminate against or exclude any woman for her political affiliations.

Zel Andrews, New York state coordinator of NOW, spoke in favor of the motion, saying she "deplored" the red-baiting resolution passed by the conference. She urged the board to "recall our statement of purpose," which declares that NOW is a nonexclusionary organization.

Shelley Fernandez, a board member from San Francisco, said that the conference resolution against the SWP "takes us back to the days of red-baiting and the McCarthy era when people's lives were destroyed."

But the board majority had no intention of rescinding the attack on the SWP, an attack they had supported. They succeeded in reversing the meaning of the nonexclusionary motion, so that it read:

"The national board affirms its support of the resolutions passed by the national conference. The board also reaffirms NOW's traditional policy that it is an open and democratic organization that does not exclude or otherwise discriminate against any member on the basis of political affiliation."

This contradictory motion, which was aimed at reinforcing the red-baiting resolution, passed.

"NOW members must urge recision of the conference resolution against the SWP," said Rhonda Rutherford. "We must bring this destructive attack to the attention of NOW at the chapter, state, and regional level."

In the final caucus meeting of Defending Women's Rights supporters, Rutherford had told women: "For the first time in NOW's history, we have had a discussion of strategy—how we are going to move forward to combat the attacks on our rights, how we are going to bring thousands of Black and Latina women into NOW, and how we are going to get back out into the streets again. This discussion is an important victory for all NOW members.

"Through this discussion we have explained the dangers of the opposite strategy—the perspective put forward by NOW's leadership. We have to bring this debate back to our local chapters.

"This discussion has just begun, and we are going to win."

'An attack on all NOW members'

SWP ANSWERS RED-BAITING
Reprinted from the 'Militant,' May 6, 1977

By Mary-Alice Waters

DETROIT—In the final hours of the 1977 national conference of the National Organization for Women, with only a few hundred of the nearly 2,000 delegates and other members present, a motion was placed on the floor and stampeded to a vote.

It stated that "this conference protests attempts by the Socialist Workers Party to use NOW as a vehicle to place before the public the agenda of their organization and to exploit the feminist movement. We bitterly resent and will not tolerate any group's attempts to deflect us from pursuit of our feminist goals."

In order to win passage of the motion, its sponsors had been obliged to wait until most of the delegates had left. Moreover, they used slanderous rumors conveniently circulating on the conference floor in order to whip up an intimidating lynch atmosphere.

The rumor, quickly confirmed to be false, was that women from the Minority Women workshop were holding a news conference to denounce NOW as a racist organization.

Despite outright harassment, insults, and abuse aimed at provoking a physical confrontation on the floor of the conference, the Black and Latina women present had led the debate in the afternoon plenary session urging the delegates to adopt a resolution that would commit NOW to fight for the needs of women of the oppressed nationalities. To the cheering and clapping of those delegates who thought NOW should continue to orient to more affluent white women, the resolution was defeated.

Throughout the weekend, Black and Latina NOW members were repeatedly told they were being manipulated by the SWP because they shared the opinion that NOW must fight for the needs of the most oppressed women if it is to be a viable feminist organization. They bitterly resented the insulting implication that they were incapable of thinking for themselves.

While the red-baiting motion was ostensibly directed at Blacks, Latinas, and SWP members who belong to NOW, the real target was the entire NOW membership.

Red-baiting, agent-baiting, lesbian-baiting, and other forms of witch-hunting have one central purpose: intimidation. They are used to scare people away from objectively considering all ideas and openly expressing their opinions. They are intended to sow division and discord in order to divert attention from the important questions under debate.

Real issues underneath

The conference motion did not fall from the sky unprepared. It was the final expression of a red-baiting drive that began long before the delegates gathered in Detroit. The campaign of intimidation then picked up momentum as the conference discussion revealed that many NOW members strongly disagreed with the political perspectives proposed by the leadership.

The meeting was billed as a "unity conference." But the depth of the differences in NOW was perhaps best indicated by the vote on the resolution establishing a Political Action Committee. The purpose of NOW-PAC will be to endorse and give funds to candidates for public office deemed by the NOW leadership to be supporters of feminist issues.

But the delegates were split down the middle on this proposal. The vote on the resolution was so close that the chair had to call for a standing vote and even then had to hesitate before ruling that the motion had passed.

Instead of subordinating the feminist movement to the electoral needs of some candidate, many NOW members had a different perspective for building NOW as a mass feminist organization. They wanted NOW to chart a course toward independent action aimed at mobilizing millions of women to win ratification of the Equal Rights Amendment and counter the concerted attacks on our rights to abortion, maternity benefits, affirmative-action programs, child care, and other gains of the past decade.

Instead of openly and objectively discussing out these two alternative perspectives for how to build NOW and achieve our goals, the oldest game in the books was tried. If advocating and arguing for the independent mobilization of women could be branded as an SWP "hidden agenda" and a "disruption," then perhaps fewer women would stop to seriously consider the merits of the arguments presented.

Long campaign

So the campaign of intimidation began last January, when two members of Philadelphia NOW who are also members of the SWP drafted and began circulating an alternative perspectives resolution entitled "Defending Women's Rights in the Second Decade."

In the weeks leading up to the NOW conference, signers of the resolution and other supporters around the country were subjected to an organized pressure campaign, trying to convince them to take their names off the resolution. Despite the fact that only a few of the hundreds of supporters of the resolution were members of the SWP, it was branded as "the SWP resolution."

As the red-baiting campaign gathered steam, NOW members who belong to the SWP were undemocratically excluded from being delegates to the conference in a number of cities. For example, both Clare Fraenzl and Rhonda Rutherford, the originators of the resolution, were excluded from the Philadelphia delegation.

On the first day of the conference, the May 1977 issue of the *NOW Times*, published by the Los Angeles County chapters of NOW, was distributed to all participants. It featured a full-page article entitled "SWP: A Study in Political Parasitism." Both style and content were reminiscent of material unearthed in FBI files in recent years. The gist of the article was to accuse NOW members who belong to the SWP of trying to infiltrate and manipulate NOW.

How? By openly trying to win support for a resolution that "is an attempt to have [NOW] commit ourselves to an action that by itself will get us absolutely nothing."

"We should be wary of those who would divert us into activity that consumes our time, energy, and money—without producing the desired result," warned the *NOW Times*.

How is openly advocating the independent mobilization of women manipulative?

Because, the argument goes, the SWP has ulterior motives. It doesn't really care about women's rights. It is "largely dominated by white men." Presumably, that is why women members of the SWP deviously pretend to be feminists and try to get NOW to adopt a losing strategy.

According to the *NOW Times* editors, the SWP advocates the mobilization of masses of women in action to win their demands because such activities "attract crowds and press coverage SWP could never gather in its own name. Such crowds offer SWP recruiting opportunities as well as fundraising opportunities."

Furthermore, mobilizations "build the frustration of the masses by their very ineffectiveness and presumably may make converts to the SWP and its revolutionary purpose."

The accusations of the *NOW Times* editors are false from start to finish. Leaving aside the gratuitous and unsubstantiated slander that the SWP collects money for itself under false pretenses, let's get to the real political issue.

What SWP stands for

The SWP advocates activities such as rallies, picket lines, demonstrations, teach-ins, educational conferences, and other similar activities because we believe that all historical experience has confirmed that women can win their rights only by convincing larger and larger numbers of women and our allies to join in the struggle. In order to publicize our demands and inspire women with confidence in our collective power and our ability to win, we must engage in united action that demonstrates our strength—even to ourselves.

A campaign to bring millions of women into the streets in the next twenty-three months, demanding ratification of the ERA, would have more impact on the spineless legislators NOW is trying to coddle into voting for the ERA than a million dollars spent on election campaigns, cocktails, dinners, telephone calls, and quiet discussions in carpeted chambers.

That is not only the opinion of the SWP. It is the perspective that hundreds of women at the NOW conference were arguing for.

The reason the *NOW Times* felt compelled to brand them all as dupes of the SWP, incapable of thinking and deciding for themselves, is spelled out clearly in their article. "A 'show of force' in the streets is no substitute for the exercise of political power in the next elections, and that's where we need to put our money, our time, our energy, and our organizing efforts for the foreseeable future."

Talk about a perspective that builds frustration by its very ineffectiveness!

Absent from the *NOW Times* strategy is any talk of "multiplicity of tactics," which was alleged by the leadership to be the heart of its ERA strategy. The real "hidden agenda" came to the fore in the *NOW Times*.

To win approval for this rightward course, however, the atmosphere of intimidation was essential. Even after an intense red-baiting campaign against the most outspoken opponents of this perspective, the motion to turn NOW more and more into an electoral pressure group could barely muster half the votes.

Against feminist goals?

The red-baiting motion placed before the NOW conference claims that the SWP is trying to deflect NOW from its feminist goals and use the women's movement for some other end. If such were the case it would certainly be a self-defeating perspective.

An uncompromising fight for women's liberation has always been a touchstone of our program and politics. We believe an independent mass feminist movement must be built. We believe that women must organize to fight for their needs and their demands. We state our goals and our strategy openly. If anyone has any doubts they need only read our resolutions, articles, pamphlets, and books.

If SWP members were trying to deflect NOW from the pursuit of feminist goals, we would be deflecting ourselves.

It is not the common goals shared by all NOW members that are at issue, but what course of action must be followed to achieve them.

After the conference Eleanor Smeal told the press that the "problem" at the conference was not the SWP's ideas, but its "tactics." Unfortunately, she had the source of the problem misplaced.

It was evident to all that there was something seriously amiss at the NOW conference. The treatment afforded Black and Latina NOW members was outrageous. (Some were even stopped at the door and asked to produce special identification!)

Workshops were designed to prevent any discussion on the perspectives before NOW. Hours and hours of plenary time were wasted on trivia and parliamentary maneuvering. Officers were elected on the basis of petty personality contests, not their programs for building NOW.

Then there was the campaign to place an SWP label on any woman who was disturbed by all this and had some ideas of her own about the kind of organization NOW should be. The result was an atmosphere in which no real democratic discussion could take place.

The goal of hundreds of women present at the conference, including NOW members who belong to the SWP, was to have a democratic conference that discussed and decided the real questions. That was our "tactic." The source of the problem at the NOW conference was the "tactics" of those who were determined to prevent a full and democratic discussion from taking place.

To decide upon a correct course of action to build the feminist movement we must have a democratic organization in which all members are able to present their ideas as convincingly and as effectively as possible, without fear or intimidation. Democracy is not a moral question, but an organizational and political imperative if we are to be able to pool all our experiences and abilities, discuss the alternatives before us, and arrive at the correct course of action.

That is why racism, red-baiting, agent-baiting, lesbian-baiting, and similar attempts to divide women against each other only hurt NOW and cut across our ability to pursue our feminist goals. They are aimed at creating a category of second-class members, whose ideas should not be considered on their merits.

Such tactics of divide and destroy are as old as the oppression of women and serve no one but our enemies.

Only a handful of NOW's 55,000 members voted for the red-baiting attack on their own organization at the close of the conference. We are confident it does not represent the opinion of the organization as a whole. The overwhelming majority of NOW members are determined to preserve the democratic foundations on which NOW has been built, and they will make that opinion heard in the months to come.

CAMPAIGNING FOR THE ERA
IMPACT OF THE JULY 9, 1978, 100,000-STRONG MARCH ON WASHINGTON FOR THE ERA AND THE PERSPECTIVES FOR NOW
Report adopted by SWP Political Bureau, November 3, 1978

by Wendy Lyons

This year's conference of the National Organization for Women showed that significant changes are taking place in the organization which reflect a shift in the broader political situation the party faces.

The ruling-class campaign to drive down the standard of living and rights of all working people is now meeting with resistance. The 110-day coal strike marked the beginning of a new mood of militancy and willingness to fight back. The victorious fight for the extension of the ERA ratification deadline was part of this new resistance.

The NOW conference showed that women are becoming more concerned with broad political questions under the impact of the rulers' attacks and the growing response against them. Many NOW members saw the need to make alliances with the labor movement and Black and Latino organizations in a common fight for justice, and there was a growing feeling that mass actions are an effective method of struggling for women's rights.

To see how much progress this represents it is useful to look back at the reaction to the strategy we and others who became part of the Defending Women's Rights caucus put forward at the 1977 conference.

Needed strategy

To combat the ruling-class offensive against women's rights we said it was necessary for NOW to:

• Fight for the rights of the most oppressed women and win Black, Latina, and other working women to the ranks and leadership of NOW.

• Forge alliances with the labor movement and the organizations of the oppressed nationalities.

• Chart a course of action including mass demonstrations, picket lines, and speak-outs—actions that would rely on the independent power of women and their allies rather than the capitalist politicians.

These proposals, which remain the necessary strategy for NOW, won a favorable response from only a small minority of the 1977 conference. Among those most favorable were Black and Latina women who were being hit hardest by the attacks.

But a majority of the gathering was not yet convinced that there was an offensive taking place against women and other working people. In fact the opposite idea was put forth by sections of the central leadership of NOW. A theme of the 1977 conference was that women's rights were pretty much won except for the ERA. Now it was time to go on to win the ERA and use the rights women have won to gain influence in capitalist electoral politics. Political action committees were instituted for the first time.

While the majority of the 1977 conference did not yet recognize the government offensive against women's rights, they felt the pressure of the government-inspired campaign against the ERA. The NOW leadership's response was to back away from issues such as abortion rights and forced sterilization, for fear that association with such "controversial" issues could jeopardize support for the ERA.

A similar retreat was seen in response to the right-wing campaign to pin the "antifamily" label on the women's rights movement. The NOW leadership reacted by glorifying the role of "homemakers" and housework. Eleanor Smeal, who was elected president at the 1977 conference, pledged a major effort to recruit housewives as the backbone of NOW, stressing her own credentials as a "homemaker."

In the year and a half between the 1977 and

1978 conferences two things happened that profoundly affected the thinking of NOW members and masses of other women. On the one hand the attacks against women and all working people intensified; on the other, decisive sectors of the working class began to fight back against the attacks and win some victories, inspiring others to follow suit.

After the 1977 conference the attacks against women came fast and furious:

• Poor women were denied abortions when the Hyde amendment went into effect cutting off government monies for abortions. A new round of restrictive state laws began to curtail abortion rights for all women.

• Gay and lesbian rights were dealt a blow in Dade County, Florida and later in other cities with the defeat of antidiscrimination ordinances.

• The *Bakke* decision was handed down by the Supreme Court after a vicious ruling-class propaganda campaign against affirmative action.

• The pitifully inadequate child care that existed continued to be cut back.

Finally as the March 1979 deadline for ratification of the ERA approached, it became clear that through the backstabbing of the capitalist politicians the amendment was going down to defeat.

All these attacks against women were taking place in the context of the broader ruling-class offensive aimed at all working people. The rulers had carefully calculated, beginning the attacks with the most oppressed and least organized to fight back. This included the major assault on the public employees unions begun in New York City. Emboldened by the virtual lack of response to these initial attacks from the organized labor movement, the rulers then decided to take another, bigger step—to attack an established industrial union to probe the possibility of breaking its power. They targeted the United Mine Workers, which they considered to be the most vulnerable. But here the rulers miscalculated.

The miners fight back

Through measures of union democracy that the miners had fought for earlier and won, they were able to use a portion of the vast potential power of their union to stalemate the bosses' attempt to break them.

Because the membership of the miners' union had the right to decide on their contract and were using that power to reject deals made between the Arnold Miller leadership and the bosses, attention focused on them.

A dramatic confrontation took place in front of the whole American population. Night after night rank-and-file miners were interviewed on television explaining why they were refusing government back-to-work orders. They were able to tell their side of the story and win sympathy and active support for the justice of their cause. The miners' stand inspired everyone who was under attack.

The later actions of the postal workers and rail workers showed that the miners were no exception. Fueled by the miners' example, there was a new mood of willingness to fight back.

This was reflected in a whole series of protests. Last spring, Washington, D.C. was the scene of large marches to free the Wilmington Ten, protest the *Bakke* decision, demand jobs for youth, and in solidarity with the freedom fighters in southern Africa. The majority of marchers were Black.

Last spring we also saw large demonstrations against nuclear power and weapons—the largest antiwar protests since the U.S. government withdrew from Vietnam. Struggles against university investments in South Africa swept many campuses involving thousands of white and Black students.

In this atmosphere, and with the imminent defeat of the ERA looming, the NOW membership was anxious to act. This impelled the NOW leadership to issue the call for women and men to march on Washington for the ERA July 9.

The broad backing for the march—especially from the unions—and the massive outpouring approaching 100,000 demonstrators was dramatic testimony to the depth of support and willingness to fight for women's rights. The action also showed that the fight for the ERA had become a symbol for many—a place to stand up and say, "Enough!"

In the face of this show of strength, the ruling class was forced to pull back and concede extension of the deadline for ratification of the ERA. The rulers had had no intention of allowing extension to pass until the mass mobilization. They fear adding an amendment to the constitution that raises the expectations of women that they will get equal pay, job opportunities, and extended rights. This doesn't fit in with the rulers' campaign to intensify the exploitation of the working class, to drive down its standard of living.

Raising women's hopes that they will improve their situation and gain new rights cuts across the austerity mentality the rulers are trying to impose on the whole working class.

At the NOW conference, Eleanor Smeal and others explained how the congressional vote was stacked against extension until the last minute. The Democratic-controlled 95th Congress rejected virtually every other proposal put forward by organized labor.

ERA is victory for all

But the rulers had to reevaluate their options when they saw the outpouring on July 9. Passing the extension became a lesser evil for them than fueling the mood of militancy among women in a situation of growing protests on the job and around other social issues.

Winning the extension was a crucial victory for women that gives them renewed confidence to continue fighting. The demonstration clearly showed that supporters of women's rights—not government-inspired right wingers like Phyllis Schlafly—speak for the majority.

The concession on the ERA and the way it was wrested from the government was also a victory for the whole working class. It helped show that it is possible to fight back and win and it set an example of how to win—by mobilizing the power of our numbers independent of the government.

While NOW organized the action that won the extension, it was the 110-day strike by the coal miners that altered the political climate and began to create the stand-up-and-fight-back atmosphere that set the stage for the victory.

As Willie Mae Reid explained in a report on women's liberation perspectives at the February 1978 meeting of the SWP National Committee, occurring in the midst of the miners' strike:

"As far as the women's liberation movement is concerned, the most important thing happening in the country today is the coal miners' strike. The miners' resistance to the operators' offensive and the outcome of that battle will have an impact on winning the ERA, reclaiming abortion rights for all women, securing affirmative-action programs and other women's rights. . . ."

The changed political situation and the role of NOW in helping to bring it about has had an impact on the thinking of the organization from top to bottom.

Changes are occurring that help reinforce the efforts of those forces in NOW who are fighting for NOW to be an effective and unwavering movement for women's rights—a movement that will encompass oppressed and exploited women and ally itself with the struggles of the working class as a whole.

The 1978 NOW conference was highly political compared to the last one. More political discussion took place on the floor of the plenaries, and very lively debate occurred at workshops. While many of last year's workshops tended to be consciousness-raising or countercultural self-help seminars, this year the workshops dealt with the political issues facing the women's movement.

New view of labor

The biggest change reflected at the conference was the attitude of NOW members to the labor movement. While last year's conference held up "homemakers" as the most important section of society to win over, this year a theme of the gathering was the need to ally with labor.

This is a big shift in consciousness for the present women's movement, which was born during the quiescence of the labor movement and tended to look on it with hostility—a hostility that was often provoked by the antiwomen policies of the labor bureaucracy.

Today, under pressure from the attacks against labor and women's rights, the national leadership of NOW and some top union officials are seeking an alliance for the purpose of trying to gain greater influence over capitalist politicians. Regardless of the aims of the leadership in seeking such an alliance, their moves reinforce a positive attitude toward the labor movement among the NOW membership.

On the one hand, this new attitude stems from a growing understanding that the enemies of women's rights are the same as the enemies of labor's rights. On the other, it is testimony to the attractive power of the union movement when it begins to fight. Other layers of society begin to look to it, are inspired by its power, and follow its lead. Women have been affected by the power they saw displayed in the strikes that have taken place and they saw how important labor's support was in the drive to win extension of the ERA deadline.

This new consciousness was seen at the conference in the presence of trade-union leaders as keynote speakers, in the labor workshops that were held, and by the overwhelming support the labor-workshop resolution received from the gathering.

The political changes that have taken place in the last year have had an impact on the thinking of many NOW members on other questions as well. There is more agreement on the need to ally with the Black and Latino movements. This too was reflected in the list of speakers at the conference, which included Coretta Scott King, who received a standing ovation upon arrival, and Elisa Sanchez, president of the Mexican-American Women's National Association. In addition, Veronica Murdock, president of the National Congress of American Indians, spoke.

The discussion on sterilization abuse also indicated progress. While the majority of delegates voted against supporting a thirty-day presterilization waiting period to guard against forced sterilization, NOW went on record against sterilization abuse. In addition quite a few women were won to the position that a thirty-day waiting period is necessary to help prevent victimization of women of the oppressed nationalities at the hands of racist, sexist doctors. This support was impressive considering there is confusion around this issue and many were hearing the pros and cons for the first time.

Advances were made in winning women to see the need to fight around other issues besides the ERA. A resolution was passed calling for coordinated pro-abortion rights actions across the country on the weekend of January 20–21—the anniversary of the Supreme Court decision legalizing abortion.

At this conference many NOW members were also quick to back defense of affirmative-action programs. There was overwhelming support for the fight against Brian Weber's challenge to affirmative action on the job.

There is also greater agreement on the need to oppose attacks on gay and lesbian rights.

Cheers for action

Many NOW members are becoming partisans of mass actions. Cheers rang out when keynote speakers made references to the march on Washington, reflecting the understanding of many that the action played a decisive role in winning extension of the ratification deadline.

This helped the discussion at the conference in other areas. It was in large part because of the July 9 protest that women saw more clearly the need for allies in the labor movement and among the oppressed nationalities, making it easier to argue that NOW must reach out to and win these forces to the organization.

The desire to forge links with the labor movement is being reinforced by moves of some of the top labor officials to reach out to the women's movement, such as Douglas Fraser of the United Auto Workers union with his attempt to put together a new liberal, labor, Black, and women's rights coalition. While the labor officials and some of the central leaders of NOW see reforming the Democratic Party as the major purpose of such a coalition, the talk of alliances combined with the objective need for women to gain the support of the labor and Black movements in the fight for their rights, is opening the eyes of many NOW members.

There is now greater opportunity to discuss what kind of *strategy* is needed for the alliance of women, labor, and the oppressed nationalities to win. Many women will see the need for a fighting alliance that relies on its own power instead of collaboration with the very forces responsible for oppression and exploitation.

The experience of July 9 gave many women a glimpse of the potential power of united independent action. While many NOW members presently accept the need for mass action as a means of winning women's rights, the majority does not yet see a contradiction between this and a strategy that includes relying on capitalist politicians by lobbying or backing capitalist candidates. Rather, they think that actions as well as involvement in capitalist politics are effective ways to win women's rights.

This mistaken idea is fostered by the central

leadership of NOW. Their strategic view of how women's rights can be won stands in the way of their leading an uncompromising fight for women's equality. They believe that the capitalist system can grant genuine equality for women—that the institutions of this society can be restructured to accomplish this. This leads them to collaboration with or reliance on the very forces responsible for the oppression of women.

One form this takes, among others, is reliance on the capitalist politicians to win women's rights. When the central leadership of NOW talks about women needing more political power they mean running more women as candidates of the capitalist parties and wheeling and dealing with elected capitalist politicians. The central NOW leaders share the narrow class-collaborationist view of the labor bureaucracy in this respect.

They have driven deeper in this direction since the last convention. The national ERA strike force set up at the last conference has been organizing NOW chapters in various states to focus on capitalist electoral politics, and more candidates than ever have been endorsed by NOW chapters.

The logic of this can be seen in what happened in the Phoenix chapter leading up to the elections. The primary activity of the chapter had been phoning registered voters to tell them who the Democratic and Republican candidates are who say they support the ERA. Members have dropped away from activity due to this uninspiring perspective.

In the game of "practical politics" put forward by the national NOW leadership, women's rights are sacrificed. Women are urged to work for the defeat of ERA opponents and elect "pro-ERA" politicians regardless of their views on other issues, including issues crucial to women such as abortion rights.

The invitation to Senator Edward Kennedy, a staunch opponent of abortion rights, to be a keynote speaker at the NOW convention symbolized this approach.

The orientation of the NOW leadership puts pressure on them to function more and more as a small select group that can map out political strategy and make deals with politicians. With this perspective, the participation of the membership in decision making becomes a liability. This leads the leadership into attacking the democratic rights of the membership.

Part of that attack is the red-baiting campaign against socialists. The purpose of this campaign is to try to prevent and cloud over discussion on alternative strategy. But there is great resistance in NOW to the moves to curtail democracy. This was shown at the conference by the overwhelming rejection of the NOW leadership's proposal to amend the bylaws so that members could be expelled for violating NOW "policy."

Red-baiting was much less effective as a means of cutting off political discussion at this conference and many NOW members are seeing that attacks on the rights of socialists within the organization are a danger to the rights of every member.

The experience of July 9 also convinced many women of the need for democracy. They were inspired by the potential they felt July 9 to build NOW into a more powerful organization. They know that in order to draw new women into active participation democratic practices are necessary.

Contradictions for NOW leaders

The need women feel for a powerful organization to fight for their rights goes to the heart of the biggest obstacle facing the NOW leadership in carrying out its perspective of relying on the ruling class and its representatives to grant women's rights.

The rulers have made and will continue to make tactical shifts, granting some concessions when they feel the consequences of not granting them will lead to social explosions. But they are incapable of changing their fundamental strategy. They are compelled to continue to try to drive down the standard of living and rights of women and all working people. This strategy is dictated by the larger contradictions the rulers face in the overall crisis of the capitalist social system.

This has the effect of politicizing larger and larger layers of women, including the membership of NOW, and propelling them into action against the attacks. This is the same process taking place in the unions and the communities of the oppressed, and as one sector organizes to protest, this encourages others to fight back.

As women became angry about the attacks on their rights and disillusioned in the ability of the capitalist politicians to deliver on the ERA, this put pressure on the NOW leadership to act, as they did in calling July 9. That demonstration in turn became part of the growing resistance to the attacks and helped inspire women and others with confidence to act.

The misleadership of the labor movement—which consists of a longtime well-entrenched bureaucracy as opposed to the newer leadership of the women's movement—is feeling similar pressure. This is giving rise to splits within the union officialdoms.

There are moves to the left on the part of some lower-rung officials, who are closer to the membership, and growing disagreements among the top layers over how to tactically adjust to a situation of growing militancy among the ranks.

The moves to the left on the part of some lower-rung officials have been seen in the program put forth by the team around Ed Sadlowski when he ran for the presidency of the steel union, and the militant stance of many local union presidents during the Iron Range and coal strikes.

Top officials like Fraser and William Winpisinger of the Machinists union have expressed in a different way the pressure they feel from the growing social crisis and the new moods among the ranks. They have responded by making *tactical* shifts within the framework of the class-collaborationist view they share with George Meany. This is what lays behind the militant ring to their speeches these days and Fraser's moves to pull together a new "progressive" coalition to reform the Democratic Party.

While the central NOW leadership shares the labor officials' political perspective of trying to reform the system, they face additional obstacles of carrying out a policy of collaboration with the enemies of labor and women's rights.

The NOW leaders have clout with the capitalist politicians to the extent they head what is seen as a powerful visible movement. When the politicians respond to Eleanor Smeal it is because she is viewed as a representative of the 100,000 women and men who marched on the capitol on July 9. If the leadership were to bureaucratize and narrow NOW into simply an electoral operation they would cut off its appeal to large numbers of women and destroy it as an activist organization. This would destroy their own base of power. NOW and the leaders who represent it would become as ineffective as the Women's Political Caucus turned out to be. This places countervailing pressure on the NOW leadership—the kind of pressure that resulted in their calling the July 9 action.

At the recent gathering called together by Fraser to discuss a new coalition within the Democratic Party, Smeal expressed the view that other methods of struggle would have to be tried in addition to working within the Democratic Party.

The continued crisis of the capitalist social system will impel more and more women to fight back, and deepen the political understanding of those who have already joined the fight. This fact and the contradictions facing the present leadership of NOW will boost the efforts of those who are fighting to prevent the bureaucratization of NOW, and its subordination to the needs of capitalist electoral politics, and other expressions of the liberal-reformist strategy of the current leadership.

Socialists in NOW

The presence of socialists within NOW, helping to lead the fight for an effective women's movement can be decisive in whether NOW becomes a more powerful women's rights organization.

Our understanding that women's oppression is rooted in this social system makes us uncompromising fighters for women's rights—unwilling to subordinate them to anyone.

Since the upsurge in activity around women's rights, the July 9 march on Washington, and the extension victory, the size and authority of NOW has grown. It is viewed even more than in the past as the preeminent organization fighting for women's rights in the country. This affirms our view that all serious fighters for women's rights should be members of NOW. It increases the stakes in the debate within NOW over what kind of women's movement is needed to win our rights.

We can expect that in the changing political situation, more and more NOW members will come to agree with the strategy we support for building an effective women's movement.

The big changes in thinking that have taken place between the 1977 and 1978 conferences show the importance of continuing the discussion within the local NOW chapters now that the conference is over.

Conference decisions

Implementing some of the important decisions of the conference will aid this process. An action focus for the chapters is the best way to draw the many new women into participation who came around NOW for the march on Washington. It will also help convince new women to join, especially women from the Black and Latino communities and the labor movement.

The conference voted to call for "coordinated local actions on the weekend of January 20–21, to be accompanied by a national press conference in support of the right to choose abortion." Many chapters have already begun discussing this important date for action. The gathering also voted to support the November 13 Karen Silkwood memorial protests and the J.P. Stevens boycott actions.

Wherever possible we also want to encourage local actions for the ERA, and continue the discussion begun at the conference on the need for a national demonstration or demonstrations to win the ERA now that we have won the extension.

We won the extension through a national effort and a national mobilization. If the women's movement goes back to reliance on lobbying and electing pro-ERA politicians, the ERA will be jeopardized once again. The same national effort and mass-action approach that won the extension is needed now if we are to win the victory of the amendment itself.

Public forums and premeeting programs can help win new women to NOW and educate NOW members around the important political issues discussed at the NOW conference. These include such things as NOW's opposition to the abortion rights attacks, the *Weber* case, sterilization abuse, and support to labor struggles.

NOW can help educate about and gather support for the fight against the *Weber* case. Forums cosponsored by local unions or featuring union speakers and speakers from the Black and Latino communities would be a blow to this threat to affirmative action.

As the most prestigious women's rights organization, NOW should make known its opposition to sterilization abuse. This is important if NOW is to win more Black and Latina women as members. There is also a crying need in the organization to educate around the facts about forced sterilization. Forums—especially those featuring Black or Latina women—could go a long way to filling this need.

Labor task forces

The national conference voted to urge local and state bodies of NOW to set up labor task forces. Such bodies could aid in organizing NOW support for the labor-related campaigns the conference voted to back. These included boycotts, strikes, and the campaign against the "right-to-work" laws. In addition, labor task forces could aid in reaching out to union women, including the many Black and Latina women who are unionists, and convincing them to join NOW. The conference also voted to sponsor a national conference in 1979 on women in unions and worksite organizing.

The increased willingness of women to struggle to defend and extend their rights is being reflected in the unions. Women's committees are springing up in some unions and in others already existing women's rights or civil rights committees are becoming reactivated to help defend women on the job. In several cases the march on Washington for the ERA was the catalyst that began this process.

Wherever such committees exist we should participate in them and where they do not yet exist we should be open to the possibility of helping to initiate them. Now would also be a good time to check out the activities of CLUW chapters in various cities.

We want to encourage members of union women's committees and other co-workers to become members of NOW, which is the most authoritative nationally organized women's rights organization.

Increasing the party's strength in the basic industrial unions will aid us in our goal of building a more effective labor movement and women's movement and forging links between both movements.

Campus women too are taking action against their oppression. Thousands marched on Washington for the ERA, July 9. On some campuses women are members of NOW campus task forces or campus NOW chapters. On others women have come together around a particular issue or have formed unaffiliated campus women's liberation organizations, or women's centers.

We want to participate in the women's rights organizations that exist on campuses, regardless of the forms, putting forward our strategy for winning women's rights. We want to explain to campus feminists the importance of linking up with forces beyond the campuses in order to wage an effective fight. Central to this will be encouraging campus women to join NOW, and urging unaffiliated campus women's liberation groups to participate in joint activities with NOW.

The recruitment of more trade unionists, women of the oppressed nationalities, and students to NOW will aid the organization. NOW must encompass thousands of these women in order to become an effective social movement, and those individual women who join at this time can help this become a reality.

They can help convince other NOW members of the need to reach out to unionists, Blacks, Latinas, and students, and they can be important links in forging the necessary alliances with the labor movement and communities of the oppressed nationalities.

Participating in the important discussions going on in NOW and in its activities—being part of the women's movement—will also help unionists, students, Latinas, and Black women in other struggles.

As the ruling class continues its attacks on the rights of women and all working people, and as women go through the experience of fighting back, many are looking for comprehensive answers to the cause of this growing social crisis. More and more women will come to the conclusion that the problems they face are rooted in the capitalist system and that a new society is needed.

We should do everything we can to aid these women in their search for answers and conclusions about the roots of their oppression. We can do this by seeing to it that the *Militant* and other socialist literature gets into their hands and that they are invited to our forums and classes.

We can urge the growing numbers who are coming to the conclusion that a new society is needed to truly end women's oppression, to join us in the fight for such a society by joining our party.

CAMPAIGNING FOR THE ERA
LABOR FOR EQUAL RIGHTS NOW (LERN) AND THE ILLINOIS ERA CAMPAIGN
Report adopted by SWP national steelworkers fraction, February 24, 1980

by Pat Grogan

What I want to do in this report is lay out the plans that are in the works for an ERA campaign in Illinois. After months of discussion, speculation, and rumors, we can now definitely report that the National Organization for Women (NOW) is organizing a massive march on Chicago in May for ratification of the Equal Rights Amendment. The plans call for a major emphasis on the involvement of the labor movement. There will also be a labor conference for the ERA in April which has the backing of virtually the entire Illinois trade-union movement. I wanted to lay this out in the beginning because this is what everybody wants to know: is it going to happen? I'll come back to the specifics of it.

But, first, any discussion of the present stage of the fight for the Equal Rights Amendment has to begin with a discussion of LERN.[1] Last fall's ERA campaign in Virginia is having a powerful impact on the fight for the Equal Rights Amendment nationally. The LERN conference and rally brought together in action the forces that are capable of winning the Equal Rights Amendment. This is not to say that the 5,000 people who demonstrated in Richmond in January are themselves the forces. Rather, the labor movement, the women's movement, and the Black movement together are the forces capable of winning it.

Moreover, the LERN campaign was not an alliance of labor and the women's movement in the caucuses or back rooms of the Democratic Party. Instead, LERN was a fighting, living demonstration of that alliance in the plants and in the streets.

The key new elements in the fight for the ERA is the entrance of the unions into the battle. They have made the Equal Rights Amendment a *labor issue,* tied to other labor issues. Thus the demonstration for the ERA in Virginia, led by the labor movement, was also a demonstration against the so-called "right-to-work laws" in that state and elsewhere throughout the country. It was part of the fight to organize the South, vividly illustrated by the participation of Steelworkers Local 8888 from the Tenneco shipyard in Newport News.

The LERN demonstration also dealt a blow to the labor-hating, antiwoman Ku Klux Klan and other racist forces. It was a united action of Black and white southern unionists demanding women's equality—a powerful and progressive combination.

All these things are significant because in them we get a glimpse of labor beginning to view itself as a fighting, social movement that takes up the demands of women, Blacks, and other oppressed people. This is crucial for the cause of women's rights. The fact is ERA, or any other substantial gain, will not be won except through a strategy that includes bringing to bear the power of the labor movement.

It is also crucial for the labor movement, which will not be able to move forward unless it shows it is willing to champion the demands of Blacks and women. It would be impossible, for example, to conceive of a successful organizing drive in the South without the labor movement taking such stands, given the percentage of Blacks and women in the work force.

The LERN campaign put enormous pressure

---

1. On August 12, 1979, a broad conference of representatives of the Virginia labor movement meeting in Richmond launched a statewide action and education campaign for ERA ratification that won national support. Virginia is one of fifteen states that has not ratified the ERA. It culminated in a march and rally of more than 5,000 unionists and other pro-ERA forces in Richmond, January 13, 1980. The campaign was called Labor for Equal Rights Now—LERN.

on the leaders of NOW and the labor movement nationally. In the discussions in Chicago, and all around Illinois, about how to win ratification here, time and time again we hear, "If they could do that in Virginia, we can do it in Illinois. That's what we've *got* to do here."

LERN embodied a powerful strategy that appeals to most people who want to get the Equal Rights Amendment passed. At the LERN conference in August this strategy of uniting labor, the women's movement, and civil rights organizations in a campaign of education and mass action independent of the Democratic and Republican parties was debated against that of electing "pro-ERA" legislators. We saw that, given the opportunity in a democratically organized gathering, as the LERN conference was, people opted enthusiastically for it. It didn't mean the majority of participants had suddenly given up all their illusions in the Democratic and Republican parties. But presented with the possibility of a potentially powerful social movement, they supported it.

The same was true at the national NOW convention in October. The LERN campaign was tremendously popular among many of the rank-and-file members of NOW. Their sentiments forced NOW President Eleanor Smeal to put NOW on record at the convention endorsing the Virginia labor campaign. This was despite the opposition of a section of the Virginia NOW state leadership who wanted the ERA movement there to focus exclusively on lobbying.

The initiative of the Virginia labor movement met with a response in unions and CLUW [Coalition of Labor Union Women] chapters throughout the country. Solidarity actions were held from coast to coast over the course of the fall. Many who marched in Richmond January 13 were sent by their unions from other states.

Our comrades in industry had a lot to do with insuring the success of both the LERN conference and the demonstration. Many of the contingents on January 13 were organized by our comrades in steel, auto, rail, mining, and other industries.

Our assessment that the LERN conference signaled a new stage in the fight for the ERA, characterized by labor coming into the battle has proven correct. It demonstrates the depth of the penetration of women's struggles into the heart of the labor movement. We also see the extent to which women and women's issues are at the center of the struggle to transform the unions into democratic, fighting organizations.

Origin of Illinois campaign

I want to outline now what is going on in Illinois. There was a meeting a short time ago in Chicago of the ERA ratification project. This is a NOW-led organization in Illinois aimed at winning ratification. Up to now they have been concerned mainly with lobbying-related activities.

The meeting was organized in a very broad way. There were eighty people there representing many different organizations. Eleanor Smeal made the main presentation. She welcomed everybody, saying, NOW can't go it alone and win ERA.

Smeal said, NOW believes that Illinois is absolutely key to breaking the logjam on ERA and we have to go for a vote in the spring. This, she said, is because NOW fears a conservative sweep in the November elections for the legislature. This is NOW's framework for the campaign in Illinois.

Smeal laid out the plan of action for the spring. It included, of course, the 'phone banks,' the lobbying, the postcards—all the things we know really strike fear in the hearts of the legislators.

But the two key points were a national march—which they projected as being on the scale of the July 9,[2] march of 100,000 in Washington, D.C., and the labor conference. Also a student rally is set for April 23. It will be built by the ERA ratification teams traveling to the campuses.

This scenario for Illinois represents a dramatic shift in tactics. As recently as December the prevailing view among NOW leaders was that mass activities were not necessary in Illinois because they had this state sewed up. Ted Kennedy and Jane Byrne were going to get Illinois ratified for us. Since then this "strategy" has run into deep trouble and they know it. Both NOW and the labor bureaucracy are under tremendous pressure from the ranks to do something effective to pass

---

2. On July 9, 1979, 100,000 people responded to NOW's call for a march and rally in Washington, D.C., demanding an extension by Congress of the ERA ratification deadline in order to gain time to win the necessary three more states. In October, Congress passed a bill granting extension of the time limit to June 30, 1982.

the Equal Rights Amendment. That's why they've called this campaign.

While there is no formal call yet in print, the march and conference are being widely discussed and publicized. Representatives of the NOW Strike Force on campus in Milwaukee last week announced the march. The Steelworkers and UAW leaders are openly discussing and backing the drive. The UAW youth conference has voted to support and endorse the march.

The only thing tentative is the date. Negotiations are under way with the city for a permit for a Saturday or Sunday as near Mother's Day, May 11, as possible. So it's on.

We think this call is going to produce a steamroller effect. For example, the Mid-Atlantic Region of NOW has already begun organizing a train to come to Illinois for the action.

Part of the reason for such a response is because the target is Illinois. This is a major northern industrial state with a big, strong union tradition that still has not ratified the Equal Rights Amendment. It even has a state equal rights amendment that has been in effect for a long time! Yet ratification is narrowly missed at each vote. So, people are mad at Illinois because it should have ratified a long time ago. They are determined to make it do so now.

Our role

We want to throw ourselves fully into this campaign in our NOW and CLUW chapters, in our women's and other union committees, and in our union locals. We can build on the momentum of the LERN campaign. We have an especially good opening for our steel fraction. District 31 is right at the center of this drive in Illinois. This is a campaign for the whole fraction—men and women alike can be ERA activists in the unions.

Every woman comrade—especially those of us in industry—should be a member of NOW. It is the major women's rights organization in this country and it will grow through this campaign. We want to be part of the discussions of women's rights and how to win them that take place in NOW. One current example is the discussion on the draft, which I'll say more about later. We also want to be part of the activities NOW organizes.

Every woman comrade who's a member of a trade-union should also be a member of CLUW.

CLUW is on a national membership drive. Its last national convention in September was twice as large as the one two years before, and many activists in CLUW are Black, Puerto Rican, or Chicana.

CLUW has been increasingly active in the ERA fight. CLUW leaders such as Addie Wyatt and Clara Day have been pushing for a big demonstration in Illinois. They have been urging the labor movement—whose powerful potential they understand—to organize activities here like the LERN campaign. CLUW is at the center of the Illinois ERA drive this spring. CLUW chapters will be open to becoming involved in support activities in many places around the country.

We should note, too, there's hardly a single international union paper that is not paying more attention to CLUW nowadays. I'm sure comrades read in the *Militant* about the AFL-CIO Industrial Union Department conference January 24 on organizing the unorganized. Significantly, it was cosponsored by CLUW. AFL-CIO leaders at the conference projected a key role for CLUW in union organizing drives which, they said, must be undertaken to include the millions of women working under nonunion conditions.

Labor conference

Now I want to turn to the labor conference. It was initiated by an ad hoc committee of labor leaders from CLUW, UAW, the Illinois state AFL-CIO, CWA, the teachers, the Steelworkers, and others. After a lot of discussion, Robert Gibson, head of the state AFL-CIO, agreed to cosponsor a labor conference for the ERA. A letter went out to the Illinois heads of the UAW, the Mine Workers, the Teamsters, and CLUW, asking them to sponsor this conference with the AFL-CIO unions, which they have agreed to do. The conference thus represents virtually the entire Illinois labor movement.

The sponsors are determined to make this a big thing; they're talking about an attendance of 1,500 to 2,000 unionists. It is open to every union member in Illinois, as well as observers from other states and from the women's movement. Solidarity House is going to release someone to come to Chicago to work on it and has agreed to put out a huge poster.

The proposed speakers list makes it clear the

organizers are thinking in terms of having a national impact. It includes Lane Kirkland [AFL-CIO president]; Doug Fraser [UAW president]; Frank Fitzsimmons [Teamsters president]; Eleanor Smeal [NOW president]; and Charles Hayes [Coalition of Black Trade Unionists president].

Some officials who are backing the conference see it as counterposed to the march, which they do not support. But this kind of meeting for the ERA taking place just a few weeks before the march can't help but build it and increase union participation. Like most people, we see the two events as complementary and will help build them together.

The Illinois conference will be different from its predecessor in Virginia. It will not be a decision-making gathering to take any action. There may not be much leeway for rank-and-file participation. But we are much more concerned with what this conference *is*, than what it is not. If it materializes as planned, it will be a powerful show of unity by nearly the entire American labor movement demanding equal rights for women. Such a demonstration of labor solidarity with the cause of an oppressed group has very few precedents in recent times. It is just what the labor movement must do more of and its occurrence will spread that idea.

The fact that this conference and march are taking place in a presidential election year, in contrast to the posture of subordinating all social movements to the capitalist parties' electioneering, makes them even more powerful political expressions for the ERA. They are taking place when the capitalist austerity and militarization drive are coming down hard. But this is not the image you get of a period of cold war hysteria: thousands of women and the labor movement marching to demand our rights. The ERA campaign in Illinois is a real blow against the U.S. rulers' political offensive against our class and its allies.

Women and the draft

I want to spend some time on the question of the draft, the ERA, and the women's movement. This is an extremely important question and one we really have to think through.

Proposing to draft women and calling that equality is part of the rulers' overall militarization drive and an attempt to make the women's movement fall in behind it. It has nothing to do with the cause of women's liberation.

When NOW's position was originally reported in the press, my initial response was to say, that's great. It's great that NOW is against the draft for men and women. All the other things Smeal was quoted as saying about the need for equality for women in the army and the draft, while not so good, weren't very important, I thought. That is not true. They are very important—and very detrimental to the fight for women's rights.

We now have available the NOW national leadership's position in full and can examine it more closely. There is a good side to the position they have taken. Their statement starts by saying NOW opposes the draft for men and women. It cites the fact that NOW opposed the war in Vietnam. That's good. The statement echoes the general sentiment, "We don't want to die for the big oil interests."

But then NOW says—and this is the danger—if the draft were instituted, they would support the drafting of women as a key part of the fight for women's equality. This position presents a deadly threat to the women's movement and to the ERA by identifying the ERA with the draft—just what Schlafly has always charged![3]

It can only have a chilling effect on support to ERA by millions of Americans, including women, who are for equal rights for women but who are opposed to the draft. This is what Carter is cynically hoping for.

Because of its importance, we cannot sidestep the issue by dissolving the question of drafting women into our general position of opposition to the draft. We have to come to grips squarely with the issue of drafting women. NOW says they're for it; we say we're against it.

NOW's opposition to the draft is in the framework of their overall support to the U.S. military. The NOW leaders agree with Carter that women and the army are good for each other. Their statement portrays army life as another arena of nontraditional employment that women are breaking into. They want to use the power of the women's movement to demand that the Pentagon be an equal opportunity employer. Their opposition to

---

3. Phyllis Schlafly, a right-wing bigot, heads the national organization called STOP ERA.

the draft is subordinate to this goal.

NOW leaders say they oppose the draft because the volunteer force has proven "less sexist" than the former draftee army. Thus, more women are in the military now, and holding higher positions than before 1973, when the draft was ended under the pressure of antiwar sentiment.

This new status of women in the military has been attained, says NOW, because the sexist barrier, *i.e.,* the draft, to their entering the army has been lifted. Thus they conclude any reinstitution of the draft must be extended to include women "equally."

What is our attitude to women in the army, regardless of the draft? We are against it, just as we are against women being cops or anybody being cops. We're against cops and we're against the U.S. military because we know what role it plays: world cop for imperialism. You cannot simply ignore the class question, which is the heart of the issue of the draft.

We agree with NOW that the military has no right to discriminate against women who are in the services. The women's movement should defend our sisters in uniform from the institutionalized sexism fostered by the brass.

NOW says discriminating against women in the military means denying "our country" the talents of women and, therefore, the best possible "national security." But "national security" is a code name for aggression on the part of U.S. imperialism. The role of the U.S. military is to attempt to crush the world working-class revolution. Its purposes are absolutely counterposed to the interests of the working class and the women's movement.

You simply can't separate the question of the draft from the question of the purpose of the draft and the purpose of U.S. wars. NOW's statement waxes eloquent about women's martial capabilities: we're the best defenders; we can fight as hard as anybody; small and agile people make good fighters, etc. In the absence of opposition to U.S. war aims, this becomes a panegyric to imperialist militarism.

U.S. imperialism with its military might is the chief obstacle on a world scale to the liberation of women from the reactionary social structures that oppress and exploit us. The interests of women lie in dismantling this machine—not in our becoming a part of it.

Instead of demanding to be drafted "equally"—if there is a draft—women should be in the forefront of the antidraft movement, as many already are. We want to do everything we can to bring the women's movement into the March 22 march and rally against the draft, for example.

Draft = equality?

Now, let's take a look at this question of equality. Equality refers to a right. Being drafted—and a draft call implies force behind it, that is, the threat of imprisonment—is not a right that has been systematically denied to a certain part of the population, that is, females. Nor is it a right that is sometimes denied young male workers, that is, in times of peace: we took your right away to be drafted. This is nonsense and has nothing to do with equality. There is no such thing as a right to be forced, under threat of imprisonment, to fight and even die in a war which is totally opposed to your interests.

It reminds me of an incident at the Gary works where a young woman was killed recently due to particularly negligent circumstances caused by the company. Afterwards, an official got up at the union meeting and said, well, women want equal rights to work here. They've got to accept equal rights to die. This is the same kind of argument. But dying because of negligence of the company is not a right, for men or women.

It is also not a privilege not to be drafted into a war in which we have no interests. The ACLU has announced if the draft is reinstituted and women are not included, they will file a suit against it. Now, think about it. They are not talking about filing a suit against the draft, which is what is needed. But actually they are talking about going further than the ruling class itself would be going in the event of a men-only draft call. They're saying, women *must* be drafted. That is absolutely dead wrong. We would oppose any such lawsuit or way of thinking.

Our opposition to drafting women has nothing to do either with hesitations about the ability of women to go into combat. The Chicago women's liberation director recently attended a NOW meeting where this question was being discussed. She hit the nail on the head with a very simple presentation which made sense to many of the new, young women there. She said, we know women can fight—and they do fight when it's in their interests. She pointed to Iran, Nicaragua, and Vietnam. It is not a question of the ability of women to be combative. The question is, whose war is this? In whose interests is this war drive?

We have to be crystal clear on these questions, and discussing them has to be part of our campaign in building for the spring actions against the draft and for the ERA. We want to try to reverse NOW's position on drafting women. We strongly suspect the leadership's position will be unacceptable to many feminist fighters.

The final point is this. We shouldn't jump too much ahead of ourselves. We shouldn't begin saying things like, well, okay, if women are drafted, and we get in the army, we'll be the best fighters against the brass. We have to start from the position that the draft has not yet been reinstituted. We have to direct all our attention to the fight to stop it from being reinstituted. We may not be able to prevent it. But that's our fight now.

CAMPAIGNING FOR THE ERA

MORTAL BLOW TO THE ERA: NOW LEADERSHIP CAPITULATES TO WASHINGTON'S THIRD MILITARIZATION DRIVE

Excerpt from report on 'Imperialist Militarization and the Draft' adopted by the SWP National Committee, May 25, 1980

by Andrea Morell

Women and the draft

President Carter's proposal that women also be required to register for the draft has generated considerable debate.

Even though Congress voted not to appropriate funds for registering women, the debate is not behind us. The American Civil Liberties Union has announced that it will file suit against any draft registration law that exempts women on the grounds that it discriminates against men. The NOW national leadership has indicated that they will support such a suit on the basis that it violates the constitutional rights of women.

This debate has raised important questions that need discussion and clarification, especially in the women's liberation movement.

The first question relates to the struggle for women's equality, especially the Equal Rights Amendment, which still remains to be ratified in at least three more states. The perspective of women registering, being drafted, and fighting in Washington's wars is not popular with millions of women, especially those of draft age. This has given the opponents of women's rights an opportunity to demagogically argue against the ERA on these grounds. This, for example, was one of the main excuses cited by Virginia and Missouri legislators a few months ago when they voted down ratification of the ERA once again. "We don't want to be responsible for drafting young women," they hypocritically claimed.

While on the one hand, the proposed registration and drafting of women serves to ideologically undermine the struggle for women's equality and support for the ERA, on the other hand, it has been utilized to try to win support from women for draft registration and the draft.

The issue here is whether the women's liberation movement is going to be identified as part of the imperialist militarization drive for the sake of "equality." To do so means pitting the women's liberation movement against the toilers of the world from Iran to Nicaragua and El Salvador to Indochina.

It means pitting the women's movement against the struggle of workers at home by giving a progressive cover to the draft and the military drive. At issue is the direction of the women's movement. Which class will it ally with? Which class will the leaders of the women's movement urge women to look to: the working class, or the employing class, which is responsible for the oppression of women?

What was Carter trying to achieve with this ploy? From the beginning it was pretty clear that his proposal to register women would not get through Congress. Senator Robert Byrd and other powerful Congressional leaders confidently said no to the proposal, and there were no reports of a major White House drive on Capitol Hill to get it adopted.

If Carter did not anticipate winning on this particular point, why did he raise it at all?

The main reason was for the effect it would have in the women's movement. It was designed to divert attention from the question of draft registration and the draft to whether women should be drafted or exempted. This also posed the question of whether there should be other exemptions, for example, students, thus attempting to create other diversions and divisions.

Carter also hoped to deal a body blow to the fight for women's equality by equating it with the draft. This has long been the line of right-wing opponents of the ERA, like Phyllis Schlafly, who immediately announced vindication of her position. She told the *New York Times* that, "Carter's proposal proves what we've been saying for the last seven years, that the E.R.A. proponents want to draft women and treat them just like men in the military." This accusation, along with states rights, were the chief arguments against the ERA in the recent Illinois drive.

In a slick maneuver to win support against the ERA, Schlafly, who is an ardent supporter of imperialist foreign policy and beefing up the nuclear arsenal, helped initiate the National Coalition Against Drafting Women.

All of this helped to give state legislators an excuse to vote down ratification. Equating the ERA with the draft helped to dampen, at least a little, the widespread support that exists for the ERA. The common objections were: "They take our sons, now they want our daughters, too!" and "ERA will make drafting women mandatory. Carter even said so. And NOW leaders say so, too."

The idea that equality means a worse rather than a better quality of life is a constant theme of bourgeois propaganda to discourage women from fighting for their rights. It is the stock-in-trade argument of the employers. This seems credible to some women because of the conditions created by the economic crisis. "So you want equality? That means equal rights to unsafe jobs, backbreaking labor, inhuman hours, and layoffs."

We need to explain that the women's struggle for equality is for *better* conditions and a *richer* quality of life and that the struggle for this will improve the living standards and strengthen the rights of all working people. The same argument applies to the struggle for Black equality.

Carter wants to parlay the massive support for the ERA and women's equality into rehabilitating the standing of the military by linking it with a progressive issue. This, he hopes, could spill over to giving a progressive cast to how the armed forces are used and to the system they defend. This effort is especially aimed at winning the allegiance of women to the U.S. military forces. This is not a new campaign. For some time, the army has been featuring television commercials to recruit women. Their line is that the army is leading the fight for women's entry into another "nontraditional" area.

Carter has implied that if women don't accept the idea of being registered and drafted and serve this country on an equal basis with men, they do not deserve equal rights. Equal rights means equal obligations, he preached. This is the pressure he is using to get women to capitulate to bourgeois patriotism. This line of argument pretty clearly admits that registration today is preparing for war tomorrow.

This is precisely the same trap that some suffragist leaders fell into during World War I. They campaigned for the imperialist war effort on the basis of promises and hopes that they would be guaranteed the right to vote. They didn't win the vote right off, but the suffrage movement was split and the capitalist rulers won important aid for their war.

Let's take a look at the stand of the NOW national leadership as expressed in its position paper on the draft. This document, which appeared in the March issue of *NOW National Times*, was put forward without discussion or vote by the NOW membership. It attempts to embrace contradictory stands. It professes opposition to the draft, but advocates registering and drafting women if these are imposed on men.

In the paper, national NOW's opposition to draft registration and the draft is presented within the patriotic framework of supporting the armed forces and the needs of "national defense." They try to pooh-pooh draft registration as an effective "defense" measure today from the standpoint of anticommunism. They say, "We are told it will show the USSR that we mean business, and that it will increase our ability to mobilize. Actually registration saves only a few days. And, although it sounds strong to Americans who want to show that we are serious, in reality it proves nothing to the USSR which appreciates fully how little names on a list actually mean."

This type of argument is not new for the NOW leadership. They've used a similar approach in defending the ERA. For example, at a NOW forum in Chicago just before the May 10 ERA march there, NOW President Eleanor Smeal urged legislators to ratify the ERA as a way of winning millions of people disaffected by the Vietnam War and other social ills back to faith in "our society." Inspiring confidence in capitalism is presented as an argument for the ERA, just as "national defense" interests dictate no need for draft registration today.

In practice the NOW leadership has put more emphasis on the "right" of women to serve in the armed forces than in campaigning against the draft.

The NOW leaders favor the "volunteer army" and propose that more women be drawn into it. The *National NOW Times* features U.S. armed forces photos of women carrying out their duties. They contend that the military and women are good for each other and that women help humanize the army. The best way "to improve the quality of the national defense . . ." they argue in their position paper, "is to remove the sex discriminatory restrictions on women in the military."

They marshal statistics to prove that women in the military are better educated and less of a discipline problem than male "volunteers." This bends to the racist and anti-working class pitch of those who complain that there are too many illiterates and Blacks in the army.

They also argue that, "Many personnel categories required by the modern armed services—clerical workers, keypunch operators, computer specialists, communications experts, administrative personnel—are more readily found already trained in the female population." Thus, the jobs that discrimination has confined so many women to are used as an argument in defense of women serving in the armed forces.

The paper reasons that women should be regarded as just as good—if not better—cannon fodder than men. They cite the good combat capacities of women and point out that in many situations small, agile people are more suitable for certain military tasks. Moreover, they contend that physical characteristics are not the key to most noncombat situations and even to many combat situations. They say that "the person who pushes the button may be in a combat role, but does not require extraordinary strength to carry out her/his duties."

This is their most cynical argument. Under the guise of defending women's combat capacities, which have been incontestably proven by millions of women fighting in scores of countries, the NOW leaders try to create the impression that wars aren't so dangerous anymore, at least for U.S. soldiers. But there are no push-button wars, except for the generals. More than 50,000 American soldiers died in Vietnam and tens of thousands more were disabled for life. A U.S. invasion of Iran, El Salvador, or any other country would mean many battle casualties.

Even if the NOW leaders were factually correct—that all GIs had to do was push buttons—that scarcely justifies either men or women being drafted. Who would they fire the missiles at? Who would they bomb? They would be fighting workers and other toilers like themselves. It's the political objectives of U.S. imperialist foreign policy and the use of its military forces that is the problem.

Another argument they raise in defense of the "volunteer" army is that when the draft was in effect it kept women out of the armed forces. They point to the figures showing that since the draft ended in 1973, the number of women in all branches of the military forces has increased to 150,000. They argue that if the draft is begun again the stream of women volunteers will be cut off by the sexist bias of the selective service system, to the disadvantage of women and "national security." Thus, they say, they will fight any draft proposals that exclude women. If the draft is reimposed, they plan to campaign for drafting women, not just in the name of equality, but in the name of "national security." A major problem with this whole approach is that it takes the spotlight off the real cause of women's oppression which is rooted in class society.

Their procapitalist and promilitarist positions undermine the effect of their present antidraft stance. They argue that a draft would contribute to a climate of war, and that they are committed to a peaceful solution of "our" problems. But this is no different than what bourgeois politicians who criticize the draft say. All bourgeois politicians prepare for war in the name of peace.

The NOW national leaders say they see no "national defense" interest to be served by a draft now. It's not legitimate, they argue, to fight for oil interests. "National defense and self-defense is one thing; aggression for economic self-interest is quite another." But what about next year, or the year after, or five years from now? How will they define "national defense" needs then? Their position actually leaves open support to imperialist war. They say, "If there is a true national emergency we will serve."

This is an especially treacherous position. It's like that of pacifists and social-chauvinists of every stripe who oppose war in the abstract, then when it is declared shout: "National Emergency!" and use their standing among the masses as "opponents" of war to lead them into support for the war and to the slaughter.

The question of the draft cannot be separated from the class character and function of the military. The military is the centerpiece of the bourgeois state—the armed ruling class against the working class. Moreover, the U.S. imperialist army cannot fight a progressive war. It can't advance the struggles of the oppressed and exploited one iota anywhere in the world. We say, not one soldier for this army. Are women excluded? Good. It is that much less cannon fodder.

Women are hardly disadvantaged by not being drafted, anymore than they would be by not being cops. The cops and the armed forces play the same social function—they are the means of force utilized to defend bourgeois power. We don't believe that there should be more women cops or Black cops. We don't campaign around this. Likewise we don't think there should be any women soldiers, or Black soldiers or working-class soldiers in either the "volunteer" army or a draftee army. This is a different question from defending women and Blacks who are victims of discrimination in the military.

During the Vietnam War, for example, we didn't oppose the "exclusion" of many students. We did point to the 2S deferment as an illustration of how the selective service system and the army reflect class divisions in society. But, unlike the leadership of the Students for a Democratic Society, we didn't campaign to lift student deferments. Keep the students out and extend their deferments to all—that was the spirit of our approach.

We also are not trying to reform conscription and make it more fair. There can be no fair conscription under capitalism—unless the rulers start drafting only each other.

The position of the NOW leadership is in the tradition of bourgeois feminism, that is, feminists who are conscious defenders of capitalism. They see the fight for women's rights sandwiched into the limits of capitalism and *subordinate* to the defense of capitalist interests. In the past, they were often women directly from the ruling class, that is, *bourgeois* feminists in class background as well as outlook. Today, it includes many petty-bourgeois women. While struggling against the real oppression they suffer because of their sex, they identify with their class and its interests and try to imbue the women's liberation movement with their outlook. They especially detest the most class-conscious representatives of the working class in the women's liberation movement—most notably the revolutionary socialists.

Historically Marxists have united with bourgeois and petty-bourgeois feminists in the struggle for women's equality when possible. But the leadership of the movement cannot be left to such forces. The women's liberation movement must have a membership and leadership that is predominantly working class in composition and class outlook.

The publication of the NOW leadership's position paper has provoked a nationwide discussion inside NOW. The position paper doesn't reflect the views of most NOW members but many NOW members aren't clear what the NOW leadership's full position is, or how to answer it.

Members know the NOW leaders say they are against the draft, but don't realize the proimperialist, pro-"volunteer" army, and actually prodraft logic of the leadership's position. Through discussions we have shown that we are able to convince many women that the draft has nothing to do with equal rights.

One question that some NOW members, as well as coworkers, raise is: "You say that you are for the right of women to hold jobs previously closed to us, and you are against discriminatory layoffs. So why aren't you for the *right* of women to be in the army?"

Our starting point is the nature of the U.S. military forces and the purpose of the draft. To serve in the imperialist army is not like holding a job in a steel mill or coal mine. We are in favor of preventing the draft and the capitalist army. We are not in favor of getting rid of jobs in industry. In fact our slogan is, "Jobs for all!" Furthermore, being drafted into the army is not a right. It's not a right to be forced under the threat of imprisonment to serve in the class enemy's army. Nor do males who are drafted gain some privilege over women who are not.

Our objective is to prevent men, as well as women, from being drafted. If the draft is reimposed, will the fight against it be strengthened or weakened if women are included? It will be weakened. It will be harder to reverse a draft which includes both men and women, because it will mean that the ruling class has succeeded in fooling enough people to accept part of its military program in the name of equality. This would signify an ideological defeat of significant proportions.

In our discussions in NOW, we must argue also against any line that suggests women's support to the draft is conditional only upon ratification of the ERA, as if the ERA were our price. With or without the ERA, women have no interests to defend by being in the ranks—or officer corps—of the imperialist army. As an oppressed sex we have no interest in gaining our "rights" in exchange for militarily defending the system that oppresses us, because that's no gain at all. Nor will our rights be won this way, any more than have the rights of Blacks or any worker been won by serving as cannon fodder for the capitalist oppressors.

Some radical feminists have fallen into Carter's trap as well. Writing in the Spring 1980 issue of the *Freedom Socialist* newspaper, Constance Scott sharply takes issue with the *Militant's* opposition to drafting women even if registration for men cannot be stopped.

Under the subheading, "A males-only draft is sexist," Scott says, "Imperialist wars are wrong. The draft is wrong. But many feminists and radicals have come to see that *deliberate exclusion from the draft on sexist grounds is nothing less than rampant discrimination.*" (Emphasis in original.)

Moreover, she continues, "Feminists, lesbians, and gays, workers, radicals and all who oppose the draft and the imperialist war machine must nevertheless be prepared to fight exclusionary policies in the armed forces based on male chauvinism and homophobia."

Thus, by abandoning the class criteria for opposing the draft, Scott is led into a position of actually being prepared to attempt to build a movement to *demand* that women be drafted! She even expects "women of color . . . [to] be in the vanguard" of such a movement!

WOMEN'S LIBERATION AND SOCIALISM

Women in Cuba: The Making of a Revolution Within the Revolution
VILMA ESPÍN, ASELA DE LOS SANTOS, YOLANDA FERRER

The integration of women into the ranks and leadership of the Cuban Revolution was inseparable from its working-class course from the start. This is the story of that revolution and how it transformed the women and men who made it. $17. Also in Spanish and Greek.

Feminism and the Marxist Movement
MARY-ALICE WATERS

Since the founding of the modern revolutionary workers movement nearly 150 years ago, Marxists have championed the struggle for women's rights and explained the economic roots in class society of women's oppression. "The struggle for women's liberation," Waters writes, "was lifted out of the realm of the personal, the 'impossible dream,' and unbreakably linked to the progressive forces of our epoch"— the working-class struggle for power. $5. Also in Farsi.

Cosmetics, Fashions, and the Exploitation of Women
JOSEPH HANSEN, EVELYN REED, MARY-ALICE WATERS

How big business reinforces women's second-class status and uses it to rake in profits. Where does women's oppression come from? How has the entry of millions of women into the workforce strengthened the battle for emancipation, still to be won? $12. Also in Spanish, Farsi, and Greek.

Women's Liberation and the African Freedom Struggle
THOMAS SANKARA

"There is no true social revolution without the liberation of women," explains the leader of the 1983–87 revolution in the West African country of Burkina Faso. $5. Also in Spanish, French, and Farsi.

Woman's Evolution From Matriarchal Clan to Patriarchal Family
EVELYN REED

Assesses women's leading and still largely unknown contributions to the development of human civilization and refutes the myth that women have always been subordinate to men. "Certain to become a classic text in women's history." —*Publishers Weekly*. $25. Also in Farsi.

Abortion Is a Woman's Right!
PAT GROGAN, EVELYN REED

Why abortion rights are central not only to the fight for the full emancipation of women, but to forging a united and fighting labor movement. $5. Also in Spanish.

Women and the Family
LEON TROTSKY

How the October 1917 Russian Revolution, the first victorious socialist revolution, opened the door to new possibilities in the fight for women's liberation. $10

Sexism and Science
EVELYN REED

Are human beings innately aggressive? Does biology condemn women to remain the "second sex"? Taking up such biases cloaked as the findings of science, Reed explains that the disciplines closest to human life— anthropology, biology, and sociology— are permeated with rationalizations for the oppression of women and the maintenance of the established capitalist order. $15. Also in Farsi and Arabic.

Capital
KARL MARX

The best book ever written on the oppression of women, their exploitation in modern society, and the road to emancipation. Volume 1, $18; volume 2, $18; volume 3, $18.

 $12
 $15
 $20

Three books to be read as one

... about building the only kind of party worthy of the name "revolutionary" in the imperialist epoch.

- A party that's working class in program, composition, and action.
- A party that recognizes, in word and deed, the most revolutionary fact of our time:

  That working people—those the bosses and privileged layers who serve them fear as "deplorables," "criminals," or just plain "trash"—have the power to create a different world as we organize and act together to defend our own interests, not those of the class that grows rich off exploiting our labor.

  That as we advance along that revolutionary course, we'll transform ourselves and awaken to our capacities—to our own worth.

Three books about building such a party in the US and throughout the capitalist world. Also in Spanish and French.

The Turn to Industry and
Tribunes of the People and the Trade Unions
$20

Either book plus *Malcolm X, Black Liberation, and the Road to Workers Power*
$25

Special Offer! All three $30

WWW.PATHFINDERPRESS.COM

EXPAND YOUR REVOLUTIONARY LIBRARY

Socialism on Trial
Testimony at Minneapolis Sedition Trial
JAMES P. CANNON

The revolutionary program of the working class, presented in response to frame-up charges of "seditious conspiracy" in 1941, on the eve of US entry into World War II. The defendants were leaders of the Minneapolis labor movement and the Socialist Workers Party. $15. Also in Spanish, French, and Farsi.

Puerto Rico: Independence Is a Necessity
RAFAEL CANCEL MIRANDA

One of the five Puerto Rican Nationalists imprisoned by Washington for more than 25 years and released in 1979 speaks out on the brutal reality of US colonial domination, the example of Cuba's socialist revolution, and the ongoing struggle for independence. $5. Also in Spanish and Farsi.

Thomas Sankara Speaks
The Burkina Faso Revolution, 1983–87

Under Sankara's guidance, Burkina Faso's revolutionary government led peasants, workers, women, and youth to expand literacy; to sink wells, plant trees, erect housing; to combat women's oppression; to carry out land reform; to join others in Africa and worldwide to free themselves from the imperialist yoke. $20. Also in French.

Malcolm X Talks to Young People

"The young generation of whites, Blacks, browns, whatever else there is—you're living at a time of revolution," Malcolm said in December 1964. "And I for one will join in with anyone, I don't care what color you are, as long as you want to change this miserable condition that exists on this earth." $12. Also in Spanish, French, Farsi, and Greek.

Lenin's Final Fight
Speeches and Writings, 1922–23
V.I. LENIN

In 1922 and 1923, V.I. Lenin, central leader of the world's first socialist revolution, waged what was to be his last political battle—one that was lost following his death. At stake was whether that revolution, and the international communist movement it led, would remain on the revolutionary proletarian course that brought workers and peasants to power in October 1917. $17. Also in Spanish, Farsi, and Greek.

Fighting Racism in World War II
FROM THE PAGES OF THE *MILITANT*

An account of struggles against racist discrimination in US war industries, the armed forces, and society as a whole from 1939 to 1945, taken from the pages of the socialist newsweekly, the *Militant*. These struggles helped lay the basis for the proletarian-based civil rights movement that followed. $20

Our History Is Still Being Written
The Story of Three Chinese Cuban Generals in the Cuban Revolution
ARMANDO CHOY, GUSTAVO CHUI, MOISÉS SÍO WONG, MARY-ALICE WATERS

"What was the key measure to uproot discrimination against Chinese and blacks in Cuba? It was the socialist revolution itself." New edition sheds light on Chinese Cubans' involvement in Cuba's internationalist course, including in Africa and Latin America. $15. Also in Spanish, French, Farsi, and Chinese.

Socialism and Man in Cuba
ERNESTO CHE GUEVARA, FIDEL CASTRO

"Man truly reaches his full human condition when he produces without being compelled by physical necessity to sell himself as a commodity," wrote Guevara in 1965. $5. Also in Spanish, French, Farsi, and Greek.

Red Zone
Cuba and the Battle against Ebola in West Africa
ENRIQUE UBIETA GÓMEZ

When three African countries were hit in 2014–15 by the largest Ebola epidemic on record, Cuba's revolutionary government responded to an international call and sent what no other country even pretended to provide: more than 250 volunteer doctors, nurses, and other medical workers. This firsthand account of their actions shows the kind of men and women only a socialist revolution can produce. $17. Also in Spanish and French.

Cuba and the Coming American Revolution
JACK BARNES

This is a book about the struggles of working people in the imperialist heartland, the youth attracted to them, and the example set by the Cuban people that revolution is not only necessary—it can be made. It is about the class struggle in the US, where the revolutionary capacities of workers and farmers are today as utterly discounted by the ruling powers as were those of the Cuban toilers. And just as wrongly. $10. Also in Spanish, French, and Farsi.

Che Guevara Talks to Young People

Guevara challenges the youth of Cuba and the world to work. To become disciplined. To join the vanguard on the front lines of struggles, small and large. To become a different kind of human being as they fight together with working people of all lands to transform the world. $12. Also in Spanish and Greek.

50 Years of Covert Operations in the US
Washington's Political Police and the American Working Class
LARRY SEIGLE, FARRELL DOBBS, STEVE CLARK

How class-conscious workers have fought against the drive to build the "national security" state essential to maintaining capitalist rule. $10. Also in Spanish and Farsi.

Maurice Bishop Speaks
The Grenada Revolution and Its Overthrow, 1979–83

The triumph of the 1979 revolution in the Caribbean island of Grenada under the leadership of Maurice Bishop gave hope to millions throughout the Americas. Invaluable lessons from the workers and farmers government destroyed by a Stalinist-led counterrevolution in 1983. $20

The History of the Russian Revolution
LEON TROTSKY

How, under Lenin's leadership, the Bolshevik Party led millions of workers and farmers to overthrow the state power of the landlords and capitalists in 1917 and bring to power a government that advanced their class interests at home and worldwide. Unabridged, 3 vols. in one. Written by one of the central leaders of that socialist revolution. $30. Also in French and Russian.

How Far We Slaves Have Come!
South Africa and Cuba in Today's World
NELSON MANDELA, FIDEL CASTRO

Speaking together in Cuba in 1991, Mandela and Castro discuss the role of Cuba in the history of Africa and Angola's victory over the invading US-backed South African army. That victory accelerated the fight to bring down the racist apartheid system. $7. Also in Spanish and Farsi.

The Fight against Fascism in the USA
Forty Years of Struggle Described by Participants
JAMES P. CANNON AND OTHERS

In 1939 some 50,000 people in New York City responded to a call by the Socialist Workers Party to answer a pro-Nazi rally of 20,000. "The question of how to fight fascism was answered in thunderous tones by the magnificent demonstration which raised the cry: Workers Defense Guards to crush the fascist danger!" $5

WWW.PATHFINDERPRESS.COM

Also from Pathfinder

The Communist Manifesto
Karl Marx and Frederick Engels

Communism, say the founding leaders of the revolutionary workers movement, is not a set of ideas or preconceived "principles" but workers' line of march to power, springing from a "movement going on under our very eyes." $5. Also in Spanish, French, Farsi, and Arabic.

Origin of the Family, Private Property, and the State
Frederick Engels

How the emergence of class-divided society gave rise to repressive state bodies and family structures that protect the property of the ruling layers and enable them to pass along wealth and privilege. Engels discusses the consequences for working people of these class institutions—from their original forms to their modern versions. $15. Also in Farsi.

The Teamster series
Farrell Dobbs

"The principal lesson from the Teamster experience is not that, under an adverse relationship of forces, the workers can be overcome, but that, with proper leadership, they can overcome." —*Farrell Dobbs*

Four books on the strikes, organizing drives, and political campaigns that transformed the Teamsters across the Midwest in the 1930s into a militant industrial union movement. Written by the general organizer of these Teamster battles and leader of the Socialist Workers Party.

A tool for workers engaged in union struggles around wages and conditions, seeking to organize a union in every workplace and advance the fight for an independent labor party. $16 each, series $50. Also in Spanish. *Teamster Rebellion* is available in French, Farsi, and Greek.

The Long View of History
George Novack

Why and how the revolutionary struggle by working people to end millennia of oppression and exploitation is a realistic perspective. $5. Also in Farsi.

New International
A MAGAZINE OF MARXIST POLITICS AND THEORY

U.S. IMPERIALISM HAS LOST THE COLD WAR
JACK BARNES

The collapse of regimes across Eastern Europe and the USSR claiming to be communist did not mean workers and farmers there had been crushed. In today's sharpening capitalist conflicts and wars, these toilers are joining working people the world over in the class struggle against exploitation. In *New International* no. 11. $14. Also in Spanish, French, Farsi, and Greek.

CAPITALISM'S LONG HOT WINTER HAS BEGUN
JACK BARNES

Today's global capitalist crisis is but the opening stage of decades of economic, financial, and social convulsions and class battles. Class-conscious workers confront this historic turning point for imperialism with confidence, Jack Barnes writes, drawing satisfaction from being "in their face" as we chart a revolutionary course to take power. In *New International* no. 12. $14. Also in Spanish, French, Farsi, Arabic, and Greek.

OUR POLITICS START WITH THE WORLD
JACK BARNES

The huge economic and cultural inequalities between imperialist and semicolonial countries, and among classes within them, are accentuated by the workings of capitalism. To build parties able to lead a successful revolutionary struggle for power in our own countries, vanguard workers must be guided by a strategy to close this gap. In *New International* no. 13. $14. Also in Spanish, French, Farsi, and Greek.

The Jewish Question
A MARXIST INTERPRETATION
Abram Leon

Why is Jew-hatred still raising its ugly head? What are its class roots—from antiquity through feudalism, to capitalism's rise and current crises? Why is there no solution under capitalism without revolutionary struggles that transform working people as we fight to transform our world? The author, Abram Leon, was killed in the Nazi gas chambers. This 2020 edition has a revised translation, new introduction, and 40 pages of illustrations and maps. $17. Also in Spanish and French.

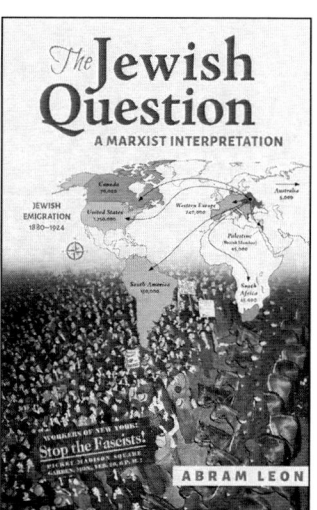

The Transitional Program for Socialist Revolution
Leon Trotsky

The Socialist Workers Party program, drafted by Trotsky in 1938, still guides the SWP and communists the world over. The party "uncompromisingly gives battle to all political groupings tied to the apron strings of the bourgeoisie. Its task—the abolition of capitalism's domination. Its aim—socialism. Its method—the proletarian revolution." $17. Also in Farsi.

In Defense of the US Working Class
Mary-Alice Waters

"Without understanding the devastation of the lives of working-class families in the US, you can't understand what's happening in politics." When tens of thousands of West Virginia teachers and school employees set an example in 2018 with their victorious strikes, they drew on the fighting traditions of oppressed and exploited producers of all skin colors and national origins. They fought for dignity and respect for themselves, their families, and for all working people. $7. Also in Spanish, French, Farsi, and Greek.

Art and Revolution
WRITINGS ON LITERATURE, POLITICS, AND CULTURE
Leon Trotsky

"Art can become a strong ally of revolution only insofar as it remains faithful to itself," wrote Trotsky in 1938. $15

WWW.PATHFINDERPRESS.COM

Workers and the US rulers' deepening political crisis

Three books for today's spreading and deepening debate among working people looking for a way forward in face of capitalism's global economic and social calamity and wars.

Are they rich because they're smart?
Class, privilege, and learning under capitalism
JACK BARNES

$10. Also in Spanish, French, Farsi, and Arabic.

The Clintons' anti-working-class record
Why Washington fears working people
JACK BARNES

$10. Also in Spanish, French, Farsi, and Greek.

Is socialist revolution in the US possible?
A necessary debate among working people
MARY-ALICE WATERS

$7. Also in Spanish, French, and Farsi.

"When we face new and unexpected challenges we will always be able to recall the epic of Angola with gratitude, because without Angola we would not be as strong as we are today."
—Raúl Castro
May 1991

Cuba and Angola: The war for freedom
HARRY VILLEGAS ("POMBO")

$10. Also in Spanish.

Capitalism's world disorder
Working-class politics at the millennium
JACK BARNES

$20. Also in Spanish and French.